Series Editor   Andy Owen   Head of Geography, The Community College,
Bishop's Castle, Shropshire

Authors
David Flint   Newman College, Birmingham
Peter Jackson   Harrow School, London
Steve Lepper   Advisory Teacher, Norwich
Andy Owen   The Community College, Bishop's Castle
Graham Yates   Ryton Comprehensive School, Gateshead

Heinemann Educational Publishers
Halley Court, Jordan Hill, Oxford OX2 8EJ
A Division of Reed Educational & Professional Publishing Ltd

OXFORD MELBOURNE AUCKLAND
JOHANNESBURG BLANTYRE GABORONE
IBADAN PORTSMOUTH (NH) USA CHICAGO

First published 1995

03 02 01 00
10 9 8 7 6

ISBN 0 435 35114 1

Designed and produced by Gecko Ltd, Bicester, Oxon

Cover photos by The Image Bank (left); Panos Pictures/Jim Holmes (right)
The photographs on the front cover show how important water is, especially clean water.
The smaller photograph shows a dried out and cracked river bed, in California, USA.
The larger photograph shows a woman fetching drinking water from a well, during a flood in Bangladesh.

Printed in Spain by Mateu Cromo Artes Graficas SA

Acknowledgements

The authors and publishers would like to thank the following for permission to use
photographs/copyright material (the numbers refer to the pages on which material appears).

Butterworth-Heinemann: 76, map by permission of the publishers; ® Colour Maps (Norwich) Jarrold Publishing: map, 73; Development
Education Centre (Birmingham): cartoons, 11, 13, 59, 83; Florida Division of Tourism: data for table, 90; The Guardian Newspaper:
extracts, 16, 31, 42, 91; Harrup Columnbus: extract, 77; Los Angeles Times: weather maps from USA Today, 84; Michelin Tyres plc: maps
36–37, 61, reproduced by permission of Michelin from their Motoring Atlas of Great Britain and Ireland, 2nd Edition, Authorization No
95–020; Jon Murray: extract, 48; National Geographic: illustration, 24, based on original image by Chuck Carter, map, 43; National Rivers
Authority: maps, 35; The Observer: extract, 61; Ordnance Survey: © Crown Copyright, maps, 60, 80; Philip Allan Publishers: map,
Geography Review Vol 7 No 4, 55; George Philip Ltd: maps, 24, 29, 65, 78; pie charts, 15, 55, 83; graph 59; Severn Trent Water; graph, 32;
Thomson Tour Operations Limited: map, 90; © Times Newspapers Limited: 1992, map, 42; © Trails Illustrated, Ponderosa Publishing
Company 1994, map, 23.

Photographs: © AirFotos Ltd: 37 (courtesy of Tees Storage Company Ltd), 38, 39B; Allsport: 21/Mike Powell; Kate Campion: 61;
Colourific: 44/Black Star/Steve Shelton, 82T Michael Melford, 89 Michael L Abramson/Woodfin Camp, 91 Michael Montfort/Visages, 93
Leroy Woodson/Wheeler Pictures; CPAT/Clwyd-Powys Archaeological Trust: 60/ref.92-C-804, 62/ref. 92-C-819; Dr Peter Evans: 35;
Doreen Fletcher: 79; David Flint 87; Ford, USA 88; Robert Harding Picture Library: 8T, 10T/B, 15B, 19R, 22, 25B, 40, 69B, 72, 82B, 84, 85;
Heinemann 42L; The Hutchison Library 8BL, 18T/Bernard Gerard, 18B/Tim Beddow, 19L/Chris Johnson, 28TL/BR, 45 all Sarah Errington,
47, 48/Liba Taylor, 49B Bruce Wills, 76B, 78/Liba Taylor, 90/Bernard Regent; Peter Jackson 54 TR/BL, 55; Steve Lepper/ Planning
Department, Norwich City Council: 73T, 75; National Rivers Authority/Southern Region: 31/Ian Goodrick; Andy Owen: 8BR, 39T, 59, 63,
64L/R, 66, 67, 69T, 70, 71T/B, 80R; Cathy Owen: 62; Steve Owen: 80L, 81; Science Photo Library: 15T/Earth Satellite Corporation,
25T/Simon Fraser, 41/NASA, 58/Worldsat International/NRSC; Courtesy of Severn Trent Water Ltd: 32; Frank Spooner Pictures:
42R/Gamma, 43R/Gamma, 49T/Beatrice Kiener, 51L/R, 53; © Michael Szulc-Krzyzanowski, 27; Telegraph Colour Library: 6, 7.

The publishers have made every effort to trace the copyright holders, but if they have inadvertently overlooked any,
they will be pleased to make the necessary arrangements at the first opportunity.

How to use this book

Location globe
This is a map of the world. It shows you where the country you are studying is.

Unit aims
At the start of each unit the key ideas are clearly set out. These are the unit aims.

Captions
A caption appears next to each picture, map, diagram, graph, and newspaper article. The ▶ points to the source the caption describes. The letter helps you to find the right source when answering the questions.

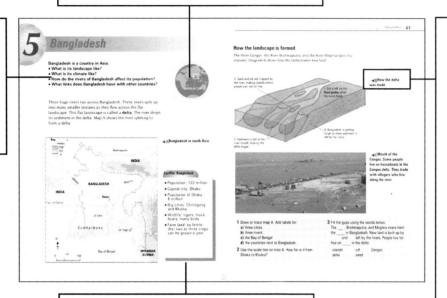

Factfile
This includes extra information about the place or topic being covered.

Keywords
Important geographical words are printed in **bold** type. They are listed and explained at the back of the book in the Glossary on pages 94–95.

Review
At the end of each unit there is a Review. This provides a summary of the key ideas you have studied in the unit. It is useful to read this before you move on to the next unit.

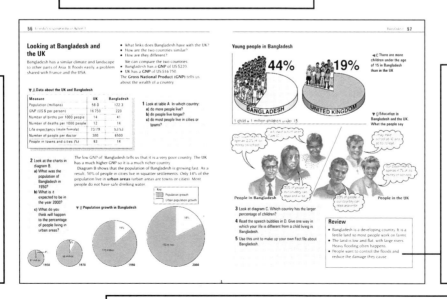

Index
The Index on page 96 lists the topics, places, and ideas covered in the book. It gives you the page numbers where they are explained or described.

Contents

Where on Earth?

1

Earth is the planet we live on. People, plants, and animals all rely on the Earth for air, water, food, and shelter. We need to look after this environment. In this unit we will be answering the following questions:
• what are the Earth's main environments?
• where on the Earth do people live?

▲ **A** *Drawing of satellite image B*

◄ **B** *Satellite image of the Earth in space*

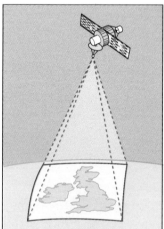

▲ **C** *Satellites take pictures of large areas of the Earth's surface*

The Earth in space

The first astronauts to orbit the Earth were amazed at the beauty of what they saw. They described the Earth as being 'like a blue pearl in space', similar to satellite image B. In fact our planet should be called Ocean rather than Earth because 70% of the surface is covered by sea. This gives the blue colour that the astronauts saw. All the people on the Earth live on the remaining 30% of the surface that is land.

Moving in closer

As a space craft moves closer to the Earth, objects on the ground look larger and more and more detail can be seen. Astronauts are able to make out the shape of continents, such as Africa or Europe. Seas, mountains, and deserts can all be seen at this larger **scale**, as in photo E. The scale of a map varies according to how much detail we want to show.

▼ D *Aerial photos are taken closer in, and show more detail*

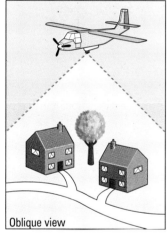

Oblique view

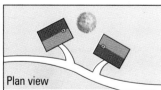

Plan view

▲ E *Satellite image of Europe and North Africa*

1 Draw a bar chart to show how much of the Earth is land and how much is water.

2 Copy and complete the following sentences about scale. The pictures on this page will help you. The words you need to add are:

buildings   large   oceans   detail

Satellites take images of .... areas of the Earth. Features like mountains or .... look small. These images are used to make small scale maps. Aerial photos are taken closer in and show in more .... features like rivers or .... They are used to make large scale maps.

3 Use an atlas to match the following list of features, which can be seen on satellite image E, to the correct reference.

| Iceland | North Sea | E9. | D2 |
| North Africa | Mediterranean Sea | H2 | C14 |

Different environments

The surroundings that each of us live in vary a lot from place to place. If you live in a city then your surroundings will be very different from those of someone who lives in the countryside. We call our surroundings the **environment**. What an environment looks and feels like will depend on many things – the shape of the land, what plants are growing there, and what the weather is like. We can divide the world into a number of environments. Areas on map E that are the same colour have similar environments.

Tundra

Areas close to the Poles where little rain falls and where average temperatures are below zero for most of the year are called **tundra**. Little grows there except for mosses and lichens. The ground is permanently frozen. Only the top few centimetres thaw out in the summer.

◀ **A** *Tundra near the Arctic coast of Canada*

Savanna

Savanna is the name given to hot, grassy plains with few or no trees, near to the Equator. Many animals such as zebras, lions, and aardvark live in this environment. Most of the year it is very dry. When it rains, either once or twice a year, the rainfall is very heavy.

▼ **B** *The savanna environment of Kenya*

Tropical rainforests

Tropical rainforests grow near the Equator, where there is high rainfall and temperatures are above 25°C. At least half the world's species of wildlife live in rainforests. The largest rainforests are in the Amazon Basin in South America and in Zaire, Africa.

▼ **C** *Tropical rainforest in south-east Asia*

1 Use photos A, B, and C and their descriptions.
  a) Which environment has the heaviest rainfall?
  b) Which environment has least wildlife?
  c) Which environment has a wet and a dry season?

2 Use maps D and E.
  a) What are the five main natural environments of North America?
  b) In which continents are tropical rainforests found?
  c) In which two continents is most tundra?

3 Make a table like the one below, and complete it using the information on this page.

	Tundra	Savanna	Tropical rainforest
Climate			
Plants and animals			
An example of where it is found			

4 Imagine you were exploring an environment you have never visited. Describe what it might be like, what you could see, feel, and hear.

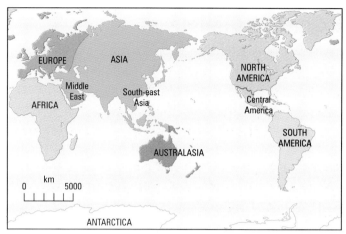

Key

AFRICA — Name of continent

Middle East — Name of region

Central and South America together are known as Latin America

▲ **D** *The names of the Earth's land masses*

▼ **E** *Major environments of the Earth*

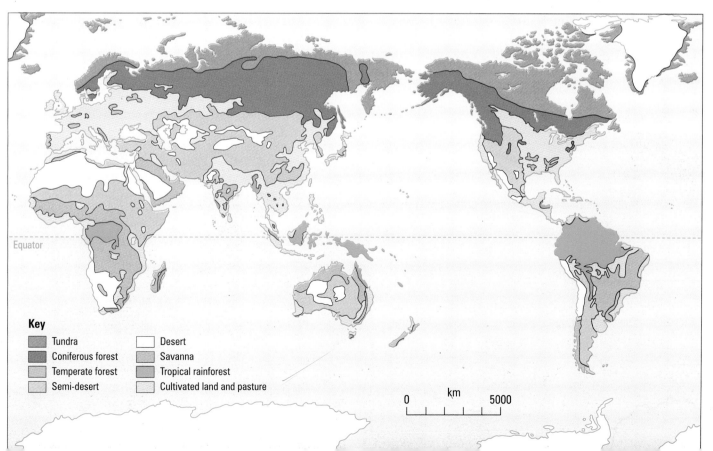

Key

- Tundra
- Coniferous forest
- Temperate forest
- Semi-desert
- Desert
- Savanna
- Tropical rainforest
- Cultivated land and pasture

▲ **A** *An aerial view of central London*

Population matters

- Where on the Earth do people live?
- How do living conditions vary from place to place?

People around the world

Nearly seven million people live in London. It is very crowded, as you can see in photo A. Other parts of the UK have fewer people living in them and those people are more spread out. **Population density** is how we describe the number of people living in an area. For example, 20 people per km^2 is the density in mid-Wales while there are 4370 people per km^2 in London.

The pattern of where people live varies all over the Earth. Many places are too dry, too steep, or too cold to live in easily, or to grow crops. However, some people such as the tribal peoples of the rainforest and the Inuit of the Arctic have always lived in difficult areas. Nowadays people use technology to adapt the environment. In Iceland, for example, people use the heat from volcanic rocks below the surface to heat greenhouses. They can grow many crops including bananas.

▲ **B** *In south-east Asia the land is steep, but farmers terrace the hillside to make the best use of the rich soils*

Population growth

In the year 1000 there were about 275 million people living on Earth. There are now over 5600 million. As map D shows, these people are not spread evenly across the Earth. The way in which people are spread across the world is called **population distribution**.

▶ **C** *World population growth*

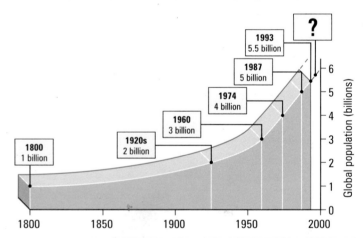

1 Use map D.
  a) Which continent is more crowded, Australasia or Europe?
  b) Which part of Africa is least crowded?
  c) From what you have learned about environments, explain your answers to **a** and **b**.

2 Look at graph C.
  a) What does the shape of the graph tell you about how quickly the population is growing?
  b) How many years did it take for the population to grow by each billion?

3 Discuss how farmers can adapt or change the environment to grow more food. Make a list. Photo B will give you some ideas.

► **D** *This map shows world population density. As you can see, some parts of the world are more crowded than others*

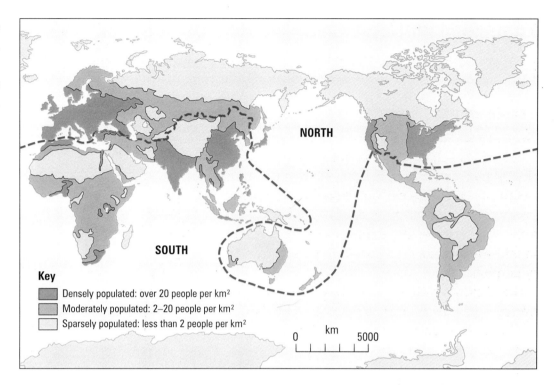

NORTH

SOUTH

Key

■ Densely populated: over 20 people per km²
■ Moderately populated: 2–20 people per km²
□ Sparsely populated: less than 2 people per km²

km
0   5000

Rich world, poor world

Just as some parts of the world have lots of people and others have very few, so some places are rich and others are poor. The line on map D separates the rich countries of the North from the poorer countries of the South. Wealth and resources are not shared equally between North and South, as E and the factfile show.

Factfile: Population and resources

Did you know ...

Only 5.5% of the world's population live in the USA, but they use nearly 29% of the world's petrol and nearly 33% of the world's electricity.

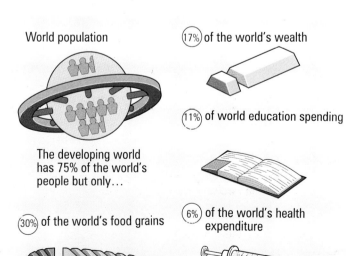

World population

The developing world has 75% of the world's people but only...

(30%) of the world's food grains

(17%) of the world's wealth

(11%) of world education spending

(6%) of the world's health expenditure

▲ **E** *Unequal shares*

4 Use an atlas to name three countries from the North, and three from the South.

5 Use the information in E to complete a table like the one below.

	North	South
% of world population		
% of world wealth		
% of world's food grains		

6 *Are all countries in the South the same? Is it a useful term?*

People and resources

- Can the world cope with the growing population?
- Does the world have enough resources for everyone?

| Timber felling | Quarrying | Factory fishing |

▲ **A** *How we use the Earth's resources*

1 Look at the pictures in A which show three ways of using the environment.
  a) Name the resource shown in each picture.
  b) How do we use these resources? Suggest one way for each of them.

2 Which of the people in B think that:
  a) the growing population of the world is a problem
  b) the use of resources is a problem
  c) a growing population is helpful.

▼ **B** *What different people think about the population issue*

3 Using what you have learned from pages 10 and 11, explain why people in the North should use resources more carefully.

(i) We need people. Their skills and talents are an important resource.

(ii) I think people in poor countries have too many children. Many of them die young or live in poverty. It's not fair for the children.

(iii) I need my children to share the work. They help make ends meet.

(iv) More people will mean more waste to get rid of. More pollution will ruin the Earth.

(v) The world is going to run out of resources. Food, oil, timber – these are all being used up far too fast.

(vi) Scientists will help solve the resource problem. They find new ways of making things more efficient, last longer, or use less raw materials.

Food and malnutrition

It is estimated that over 500 million people suffer from **malnutrition**. They do not have enough of the right types of food to give a proper balance of protein, carbohydrates, fats, minerals, and vitamins. Over 150 000 children in Asia lose their sight each year because they do not have enough vitamin A in their diet. A lot of food is grown in the South, but it's not all eaten there. Crops like coffee and bananas are sold to the North.

▶ **C** *The world's food*

Food and health

Having enough to eat is essential to staying alive and keeping healthy. But having too much of one type of food can make you ill. Eating too much protein and fatty food can lead to heart disease. Recent research suggests that some cancers can be prevented by eating a healthier diet. Graph D shows the main causes of death in different parts of the world.

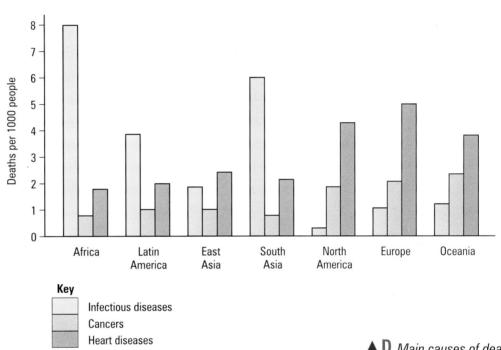

Key
- Infectious diseases
- Cancers
- Heart diseases

▲ **D** *Main causes of death*

---

4 Use graph D.
  a) How many deaths per 1000 people are there from heart disease in:
    (i) North America (ii) South Asia?
  b) Compare the main causes of death in Europe with those in Africa.
  c) How might these deaths be related to diet or lifestyle?

5 *Look at cartoon C. What does this cartoon suggest to you about how the world's food is grown and distributed?*

Review

Water covers 70% of the Earth. The Earth has different environments. The temperature and rainfall vary from place to place and this affects the kinds of plants and wildlife that live in each environment. Some environments are more difficult to live in than others. This means that some places have fewer people and others are more crowded. The Earth's resources are not equally shared among the people of the world. The North has fewer people but more than its fair share of wealth, and uses more resources than the South.

2 Life in the desert

Deserts cover 20% of the Earth's land area, but only 5% of the Earth's population live in them.
- **What are desert landscape and climate like?**
- **How do people and wildlife adapt to conditions in the desert?**
- **How have people changed the desert environment?**

The desert environment

Deserts have little or no rainfall year after year. The Atacama in Chile is the driest desert on Earth. Parts of this desert had no rain at all from 1570 until 1971. Most deserts are also very hot. Daytime temperatures in the Sahara desert, for example, can soar to 38°C. However, temperatures drop dramatically during the night.

Deserts are barren places. They have few trees and plants because of the lack of water. Few animals live there because there is so little to eat and drink, and strong winds can whip up sand and dust into fierce storms.

▼ **A** *The location of the Earth's main hot deserts*

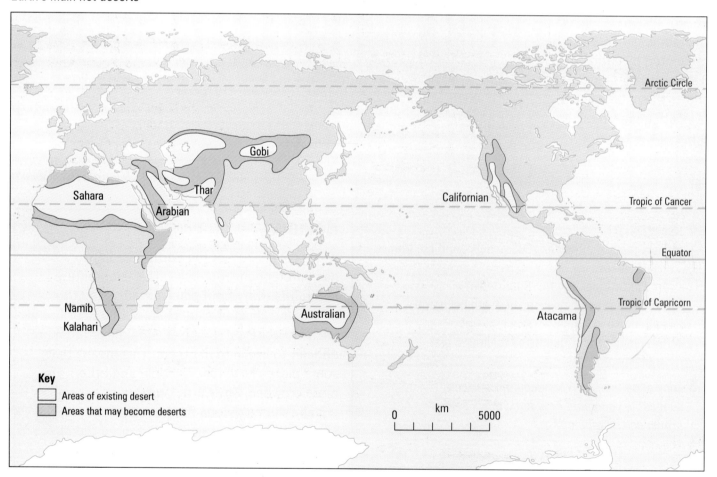

Key
- ☐ Areas of existing desert
- ▨ Areas that may become deserts

Different kinds of desert

Sand dunes can be up to 100m high in the Sahara and are very difficult to cross. These dunes are slowly being pushed along by the wind. As they move, the sand covers roads and may threaten towns, as in photo B. They may move 10 to 50 metres in a year.

Only about 15% of the Earth's deserts are sandy. In other places the desert surface is bare rock or is covered by sharp angular boulders and pebbles. Deserts are not always flat. The Atlas mountains in the Sahara are over 1000m high and Ayers Rock in the Australian desert is 300m high.

▼ **B** *A sand dune in the Algerian part of the Sahara threatens the town of Beni-Abbès*

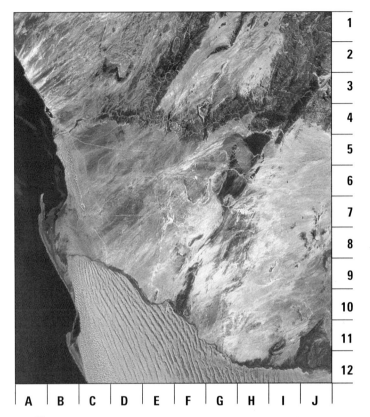

▲ **D** *A satellite image of the Namib desert. Most of the picture shows rocky desert. In the south are rows of sand dunes*

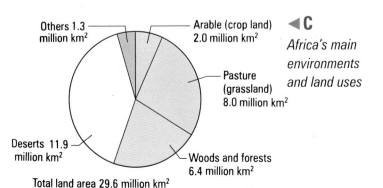

◄ **C**

Africa's main environments and land uses

Others 1.3 million km²
Arable (crop land) 2.0 million km²
Pasture (grassland) 8.0 million km²
Deserts 11.9 million km²
Woods and forests 6.4 million km²
Total land area 29.6 million km²

1 Using map A, answer these questions.
  a) Which continent has most deserts?
  b) Which two continents have no hot deserts?
  c) Describe the position of the world's deserts in relation to the Tropics of Cancer and Capricorn.

2 Use pie chart C.
  a) What percentage of Africa is desert?
  b) What percentage of Africa is forest? How might this be used as a resource?

3 Draw a sketch of image D. Label the sand and rock desert. Add the following labels:
  Sea (which is black in the image)
  Bay (grid reference B6)
  Mouth of the river (grid reference B4)

4 *Why would a desert be a difficult place to build a settlement in?*

Desert weather and climate

- What weather conditions are common in deserts?
- What's the difference between weather and climate?
- How are plants adapted to survive the difficult desert conditions?

Weather in deserts can vary greatly from day to day. In one week the weather can change from hot, sunny days with cold nights to intense dust storms which can blow for two or three days. These short-term, daily changes in temperature and rainfall are called **weather**. Longer term changes in temperature and rainfall over the course of a year are called **climate**. Graph A is a climate graph for Cairo, Egypt.

Unpredictable rainfall

One year in the desert it might rain, then there might be no rain at all for three or four years. It is this uncertainty of how much rain will fall that makes life so difficult for desert people. Often when it does rain it comes as heavy, violent downpours which stop as quickly as they started. These downpours fill the dry stream beds with rushing water and bring them to life for a short time.

▼ **A** *Climate graph for Cairo, Egypt*

Temperature (°C)   Rainfall (mm)

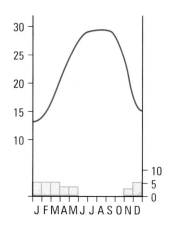

▼ **B** *Extract adapted from* The Guardian, *4 November 1994*

Flood carried flames into Egyptian village

The province of Assiut was in a state of emergency after heavy rains left more than 1000 homes destroyed. Further south another 100 homes were destroyed by the worst storm in living memory.

According to local officials, more than 125 000 people have been affected. Army and police are working together to cope with the damage, handing out tents and blankets.

Hundreds died when a fuel depot exploded in the village of Dronka. The flood water had built up behind a railway embankment. When it reached a depth of three metres, the embankment collapsed and eight wagons full of fuel overturned. The fuel caught fire, possibly from a bolt of lightning, and the flood water swept the blazing fuel down into the village.

▼ **C** *Area affected by flooding*

1 Use climate graph A to find which months in Cairo are:
   a) hottest   **b)** coldest
   c) wettest.   **d)** In which months does Cairo have no rainfall?

2 Imagine you are a reporter at the scene of the flash floods in Dronka. Prepare a radio news report. Describe the scene. Include reasons for the flood, and describe how much rainfall is normal for this time of year.

Survival tricks

Desert plants have developed their own ways of surviving with little water. Some produce seeds which remain in the ground until rain does fall. Then they grow quickly, and flower and fruit in a very short time. One African plant takes only eight days to grow and produce flowers. Desert plants have adapted to their environment in three main ways:

- by storing water
- by finding water deep under ground
- by cutting down water loss.

3 Use illustration D to help you fill in a copy of the table below.

Survival problem	Solution
Storing water	water stored in cactus stem
Finding water	
Cutting down water loss	

4 The table below shows the day and night temperature in the middle of the Sahara. Draw two bars for each month to show these differences.

In Salah, Algeria

	J	F	M	A	M	J	J	A	S	O	N	D
Temp °C (night)	6	8	12	17	21	27	28	28	25	19	12	7
Temp °C (day)	21	24	28	33	37	43	45	44	41	34	27	22
Rain (mm)	3	3	0	0	0	0	0	3	0	0	5	3

▼ **D** *How desert plants are adapted to live in the desert*

Cactus

Waxy outer skin cuts down water loss

Several tonnes of water are stored in the stem. Pleats in the stem can expand like a concertina to allow more water to be stored

Joshua tree

Thick bark cuts down water loss

Small, thick, waxy leaves cut down water loss

Long taproots go down 10m or more to find water

Creosote bush

Chemicals given off by roots stop other plants growing nearby

Roots close to surface collect all water landing there

Key
- Desert that is not used for farming
- Dry lands used for grazing
- Crops can be grown

How do people overcome the problems of desert life?

The problems of living in the desert are similar the world over – lack of rain, unpredictable rainfall, and poor soil. But people live in different ways. They have found different solutions to enable them to live in the desert.

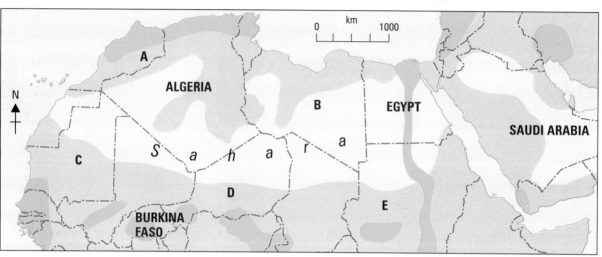

◄ **A**
The deserts of North Africa and the Middle East

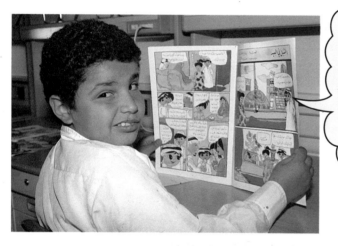

My name is Mohammed. I live in Riyadh in Saudi Arabia, in an air-conditioned flat. Saudi Arabia is short of water so we remove the salt from sea water to make fresh water in our **desalination** plants. We pump water from wells and spray it across the fields to **irrigate** parts of the desert. This allows us to grow vegetables and fruit. Other goods we have to import, like Range Rovers and other four wheel drive vehicles for driving across the desert.

Saudi Arabia
- Less than 1% of land is suitable for agriculture.
- There are no permanent rivers.
- It contains more oil than any other nation.
- GNP US $7070 per person.

My name is Kamal. I am a Tuareg living in Algeria. We wear loose, flowing clothes to stay cool and as protection from the sand and from sand storms. Tuaregs are **nomadic**, which means we do not have a fixed home. We move from one oasis to another in search of water and grazing for our camels and goats. We live in tents which stay cool by letting the air flow through.

Algeria
- The Sahara covers 80% of the country.
- 3% of land is used for arable farming.
- It has one of the world's largest reserves of gas.
- GNP US $2020 per person.

My name is Niftine. I live in a village in Burkina Faso. We build our houses from bricks made from local mud mixed with straw. Our houses have thick walls and few windows, which keeps them cool. We pump water up from under the ground for ourselves and our animals. We also use it to irrigate the land and grow wheat, millet, and date palms.

My name is Beth. I live in the city of Las Vegas in the USA. We bring water into the city from dams and **reservoirs** on the River Colorado. The water is used for industry and farming, as well as to irrigate our golf courses. We grow fruit and vegetables and import other food from elsewhere in the USA. Our farmers have built plastic tunnels to cover our crops to prevent water **evaporating** back into the dry desert air. Las Vegas is growing fast so we are having to bring in water from further and further away.

Burkina Faso

- The Sahara is spreading further into the north of this country.
- 80% of the population are farmers.
- GNP US $350 per person.

1 Use map A.
  a) How wide from west to east is the Sahara?
  b) Which country is nearly all desert?
  c) Use an atlas to name countries A to E.

2 a) Use the information provided by the four people to fill in a copy of the table below.

Problems	Solutions in			
	Saudi Arabia	Algeria	Burkina Faso	USA
Lack of water				
Daytime heat				
Lack of plants and animals for food				

USA

- Deserts cover only a small part of the south-west of the USA.
- Las Vegas makes most of its money from entertainment. It attracts 2.8 million visitors a year to its casinos and night clubs.
- GNP US $22 560 per person.

  b) What similarities have you found?
  c) What differences are there?

3 a) What does **irrigate** mean?
  b) Why can irrigation be wasteful of water in a desert?
  c) How are American farmers trying to prevent this waste?

4 *Do you think all desert countries need to use expensive technology (like desalination, or the import of expensive vehicles) to solve their desert problems? Explain your answer carefully.*

See Glossary for explanation of GNP

The Mojave desert

The Mojave desert in the USA is famous for its strangely shaped Joshua trees (see page 17), which grow nowhere else on Earth. But the Mojave is uncomfortably hot and dusty, and home to more rattlesnakes than people. You might wonder:

● who would want to go there?
● why do they find it attractive?
● what damage could they possibly do?

Having fun in the Mojave

The south-western part of the USA has become a major growth point for industry in recent years. Many thousands of people have moved into cities such as Las Vegas and Phoenix. For some, the Mojave is the perfect environment in which to spend their leisure time. One of the fastest growing sports in the Mojave is racing off-road vehicles (ORVs) or all terrain vehicles (ATVs). The desert provides the ideal environment where people and machines can pit themselves against nature. It is a fast, thrilling, dusty sport, as photo B shows.

Key

▨	Built–up area
☐	Desert
▨	Dry lakes
▨	Dunes
▨	Lowland
▨	Mountains
–·–·	International border
-----	State border
——	Interstate highway
——	US/State highway
■	Off highway vehicle recreation area
(8)	Road number

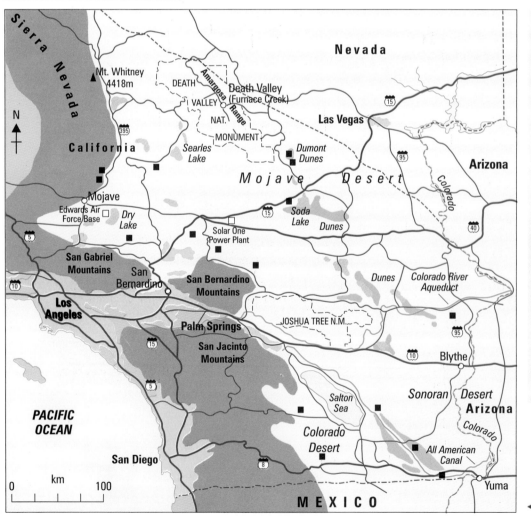

1 Use map A.
   a) In which two states is most of the Mojave desert?
   b) Name the four large cities close to the Mojave.
   c) Which river flows through part of the Mojave?

2 Look at photo B. Write a few sentences to say:
   a) why you would enjoy this sport
   b) why you might be against it.

3 Study diagram C. In your own words explain what damage is being done to the desert environment. Make sure you explain what happens to:
   a) plants
   b) animals and birds
   c) the desert surface.

◀ A *The Mojave desert*

How many is too many?

Five major roads and 40 000km of minor roads and tracks cross the desert. Special areas have been set aside for off-road racing. However, the sport is so popular that these areas are really too small. More and more people are ignoring the restrictions and using other parts of the Mojave. Diagram C shows just how off-road racing can damage the desert environment.

What can be done to save the Mojave?

Part of the Mojave was made a **National Park** in 1994 in order to protect it. However, people using ORVs and ATVs argue that they have a right to continue to use the desert. There are three main possible solutions:
● ban ORVs and ATVs from all of the Mojave
● issue permits to a limited number of vehicles
● create more areas where ORVs and ATVs can race.

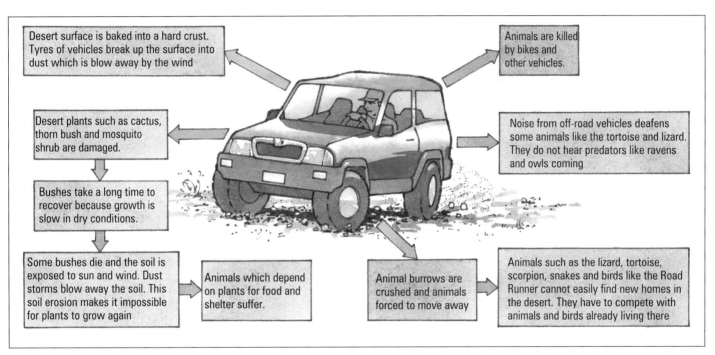

Desert surface is baked into a hard crust. Tyres of vehicles break up the surface into dust which is blow away by the wind

Animals are killed by bikes and other vehicles.

Desert plants such as cactus, thorn bush and mosquito shrub are damaged.

Noise from off-road vehicles deafens some animals like the tortoise and lizard. They do not hear predators like ravens and owls coming

Bushes take a long time to recover because growth is slow in dry conditions.

Some bushes die and the soil is exposed to sun and wind. Dust storms blow away the soil. This soil erosion makes it impossible for plants to grow again

Animals which depend on plants for food and shelter suffer.

Animal burrows are crushed and animals forced to move away

Animals such as the lizard, tortoise, scorpion, snakes and birds like the Road Runner cannot easily find new homes in the desert. They have to compete with animals and birds already living there

▼ **B** *Driving an ORV in the Mojave desert*

▲ **C** *How off-road vehicle racing affects the desert*

4 Work in pairs and say which of the following solutions you would support, and why. Consider the popularity of the sport and how to prevent the problem spreading. Use map A and photo B to help you.
  • Ban ORVs and ATVs from all of the Mojave.
  • Issue permits to a limited number of vehicles.
  • Create more areas where ORVs and ATVs can race.

► **A** *An aerial view of the Grand Canyon*

1 What do you think makes the canyon so attractive to visitors?

2 Study photo A.
  a) Make a tracing or sketch of the photo.
  b) On your tracing or sketch label
    (i) River Colorado
    (ii) river beach
    (iii) sandbank in river
    (iv) vertical cliff faces
    (v) bushes growing close to river

Protecting the Grand Canyon National Park

The Grand Canyon is one of the natural wonders of the world, as photo A suggests. This huge **canyon**, in Arizona, USA, is 1600m deep and 12km wide. It is visited by over four million tourists every year, making it one of the top four attractions in western USA.

Managing the canyon – limiting the damage

The canyon is so popular that the Visitor Centre (see map B) can no longer cope with the numbers. The car park is full from 8 am each day. There is not enough space inside for all the exhibits, talks, maps, and ranger stations. The number of visitors and vehicles is putting pressure on the park and the facilities available.

Possible solutions

There are three proposals to improve visitor facilities:
● extend the existing Centre by tripling its size and the size of its car park
● build another Visitor Centre next to the Yavapai museum on the canyon rim
● build another Visitor Centre at Mather Point, a spectacular viewpoint over the canyon.

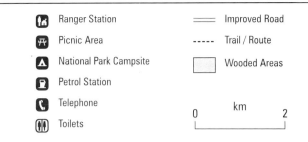

Ranger Station	Improved Road
Picnic Area	Trail / Route
National Park Campsite	Wooded Areas
Petrol Station	
Telephone	0 km 2
Toilets	

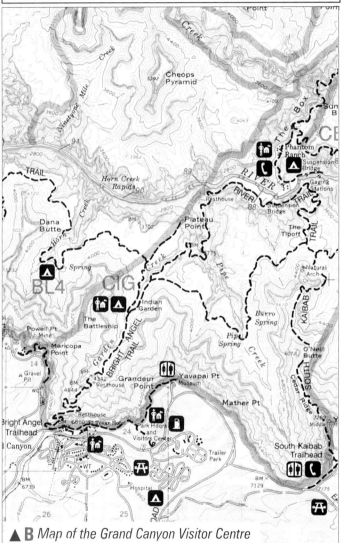

▲ **B** *Map of the Grand Canyon Visitor Centre*

▼ **C** *Opinions about the proposals*

Making the existing centre bigger will just add to traffic congestion in that area.

A Visitor Centre right on the canyon rim would have a tremendous view!

Any new development would just attract more people and cause more damage.

The best place for a new centre is at Mather Point because people arrive there first.

There should be no buildings close to the canyon rim because it would spoil the view.

We don't need more parking at Yavapai because there's already enough spare parking at Mather Point.

3 Work in pairs. Consider each of the three proposals in turn.

   a) Use A, B, and C to make a summary of the advantages and disadvantages of each proposal. The following headings may help you:

     Visual and environmental impact of the proposal

     The wishes and needs of visitors to the canyon

   b) Decide which is the best proposal. Explain why you made this choice.

Review

- Relatively few people live in deserts because of the heat, lack of water, and the unpredictable nature of rainfall.
- All desert plants and animals, including humans, have had to find different ways to survive in these conditions.
- Deserts have become popular places for tourism but this can lead to environmental problems.

Water is the basis of all life on Earth. People can survive for up to two months without food, but without water would die within three days. We will be finding out why water is such an important resource and also:
• where our water comes from
• how water is treated and managed.

Water, water everywhere...

Water covers 70% of the Earth's surface. Of this, 97% is salt water in the world's seas and oceans. A further 2% is frozen in **ice caps** and **glaciers**. This leaves only 1% available to us as fresh water. If all the Earth's water was put into a litre bottle, only a teaspoon of it would be fresh water that we could drink.

1 Copy and complete this passage.

Water covers 70% of the Earth's surface, of which ....% is salt water. Of the ....% that is fresh water we are unable to use ....% as it is frozen in .... caps and ....

◄**A** *The world's available drinking water*

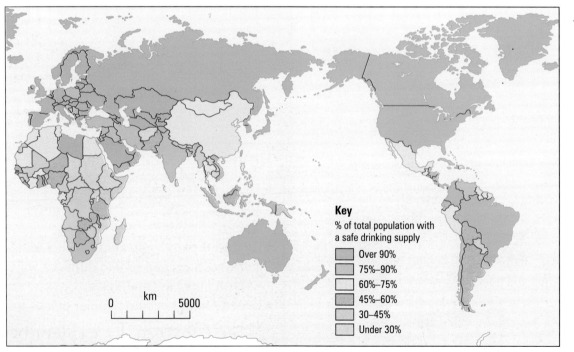

Key

% of total population with a safe drinking supply

Over 90%
75%–90%
60%–75%
45%–60%
30–45%
Under 30%

km
0   5000

◄**B**
Access to safe drinking water

Fresh water, dirty water

Not all fresh water is clean or safe to use. Map B shows that many people do not have clean water. Around 20% of the world's population, 1 billion people, find it difficult or impossible to get safe drinking water. Water often has to be collected from a standpipe, a well or waterhole, as in photo C.

A World Bank survey of water in China shows that:

● 150 million people use water which is contaminated by human waste. This causes disease and spreads worms which live in the human body. The worms eat food in the stomach, making the victim hungry and weak.

● 45 million people drink water which has too much fluoride. Too much of this chemical in the body discolours teeth and can damage bones.

● 42 million people have to walk over 1km or climb uphill over 100m to fetch water.

▲ **D** *This stream in Zabrze, Poland, has been polluted by industrial waste*

2 Use map B and an atlas to name two countries where:
  a) over 90% of the people have access to safe drinking water
  b) less than 30% of the people have access to safe drinking water.

3 Study photo C carefully. Write about:
  a) how the women collect the water
  b) why the water is difficult to collect.

4 a) Discuss how the source of water shown in C might become dirty. Make a list.
  b) From what you have read about water in China, what risks do the women in C face?

▼ **C** *Collecting water in Tigray, Ethiopia*

The water cycle

- Where does our water come from?
- Could we run out of water, or is it a **renewable** resource?
- Why does it rain?

We rely on nature to provide us with a constant supply of fresh water. The sun's energy causes sea water to evaporate, leaving the salt behind. This fresh water later falls as rain. Water is continuously recycled in this way. We call it the **water cycle** (or **hydrological cycle**). Diagram A shows water cycling around in north-east England, but water is recycled like this all over the world.

▼ **A** *The water cycle*

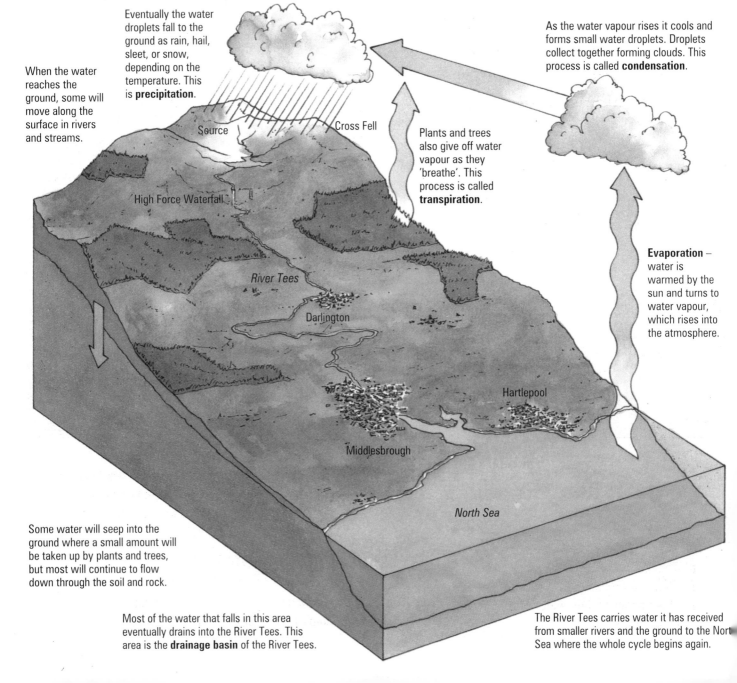

Eventually the water droplets fall to the ground as rain, hail, sleet, or snow, depending on the temperature. This is **precipitation**.

When the water reaches the ground, some will move along the surface in rivers and streams.

As the water vapour rises it cools and forms small water droplets. Droplets collect together forming clouds. This process is called **condensation**.

Plants and trees also give off water vapour as they 'breathe'. This process is called **transpiration**.

Evaporation – water is warmed by the sun and turns to water vapour, which rises into the atmosphere.

Source
Cross Fell
High Force Waterfall
River Tees
Darlington
Hartlepool
Middlesbrough
North Sea

Some water will seep into the ground where a small amount will be taken up by plants and trees, but most will continue to flow down through the soil and rock.

Most of the water that falls in this area eventually drains into the River Tees. This area is the **drainage basin** of the River Tees.

The River Tees carries water it has received from smaller rivers and the ground to the North Sea where the whole cycle begins again.

Why does it rain?

Before it can rain, moist air must cool. Air cools as it rises. When it has cooled enough for water droplets to form, then it rains. Diagrams B, C, and D show the three ways in which the air may be cooled enough to lead to rain.

▼ **B** *Relief rainfall*

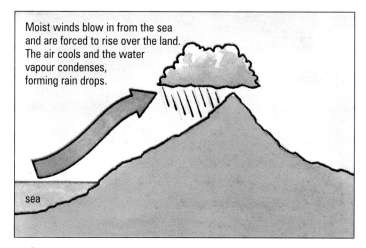

Moist winds blow in from the sea and are forced to rise over the land. The air cools and the water vapour condenses, forming rain drops.

sea

▼ **C** *Frontal rainfall*

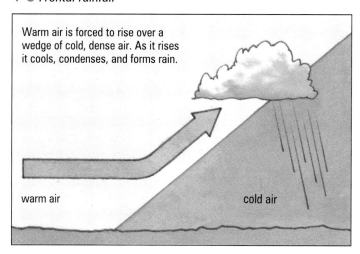

Warm air is forced to rise over a wedge of cold, dense air. As it rises it cools, condenses, and forms rain.

warm air   cold air

▼ **D** *Convectional rainfall*

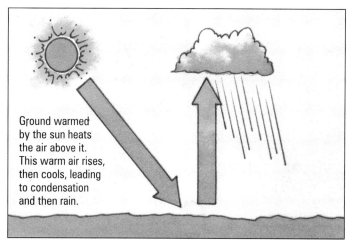

Ground warmed by the sun heats the air above it. This warm air rises, then cools, leading to condensation and then rain.

▼ **E** *Lambert Nyawera welcomes annual rain*

1 Copy these definitions into your book and match them with the **bold** words in diagram A.
   a) The area that a river drains
   b) This process occurs when the sun heats the surface of the water
   c) The term given to plants' water loss
   d) This word refers to rain, hail, sleet, and snow
   e) This happens when water vapour cools and clouds form

2 In the Arctic, water is frozen as ice. In the Amazon rainforest, it rains nearly every day. Will water cycle round as fast in the Arctic as in a rainforest? Explain your answer carefully.

3 Make a copy of diagrams B, C, and D in your book. Label your diagrams to show what is happening.

4 Photo E shows how welcome rain can be. How might rainfall affect people in different countries?

Rainfall patterns

The amount of rain that falls varies from place to place, and from season to season. These rainfall patterns have an effect on all our lives: too much rain, and we might complain about the weather, but too little, and there might not be enough for crops to grow or for people to drink.

Rainfall patterns from season to season

In southern Sudan the year is split between a rainy and a dry season. Farmers grow cereals like sorghum, millet, and sesame. In some years the rainy season only lasts three months and the dry weather ruins the crops. Farmers now plant varieties of seed that will grow quickly and can be harvested after only 65 days. The crops they used to grow took 120 days.

▼ **A** *Monthly rainfall figures for Juba, Sudan*

	Jan	Feb	Mar	Apr	May	Jun	Jul	Aug	Sep	Oct	Nov	Dec
Monthly total (mm)	5	15	33	122	150	135	122	132	107	94	36	18

1 a) Use table A to draw a bar graph to show rainfall in Juba, Sudan.
 b) Use your graph to describe when the rainy season usually starts and ends.

2 Describe the differences between what you can see in photos B and C.

3 a) Explain how the seasonal rainfall affects farmers.
 b) What have farmers done to overcome the problem?

▲ **B** *Before the rainy season*

▶ **C** *After the rainy season*

▼ **D** *Rainfall map for the British Isles*

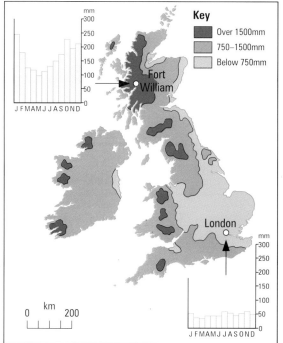

▼ **E** *Relief map of the British Isles*

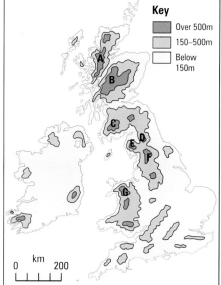

▼ **F** *Population density*

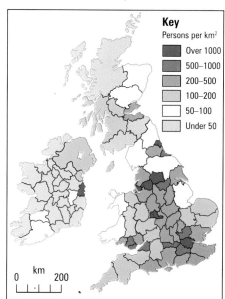

Getting water to where it is needed

When we compare the rainfall pattern (map D) with the places where people live (map F) we can see that the areas of high rainfall are not the areas with large populations. This would cause a problem if we did not collect and store water, and transfer it about the country.

Factfile: Rainfall

Did you know...

- Antofagasta in Chile has only two days a year with any rain. Alice Springs, Australia, has 31 rainy days.

- The wettest 24 hours on record were between 15 and 16 March 1952, when 1.87 m of rain fell on Cilaos, Réunion (in the Indian Ocean).

- If all the water in the atmosphere fell at the same time it would cover the entire surface of the Earth with 2.5 cm of water.

---

4 a) Which are the wettest and driest months in Fort William?

b) Describe the differences in the rainfall patterns of Fort William and London.

c) Compare the seasonal pattern of rainfall in Fort William shown in D with that of Sudan shown in table A.

5 a) Trace map E and use your atlas to name the areas of high ground A–G. List these under your map.

b) Place your tracing over map D. What is the relationship between height and rainfall? Use the diagrams on page 27 to help you explain this pattern.

6 a) Carefully describe the difference between the patterns on maps D and F (name regions of the UK in your answer).

b) What do you think needs to be done to make sure that water gets to the places that need it?

7 *Imagine that water is cut off from your home for a week; how would you manage? Would it make you feel differently about the importance of water and rain?*

Managing our water supply

As we have seen from the previous pages, water is a precious resource and needs to be managed. Rainfall cannot be controlled; it does not always fall where we want it or when we want it. Water has to be collected, stored, and transferred to the places that need it. It must also be clean and safe to use.

Where is water stored?

Water is stored in rivers, lakes, and reservoirs. It is also stored underground in **aquifers**, as you can see in diagram A. Before we can use this water, we have to remove the water from the river or aquifer – a process called water **abstraction**.

▼ **B** *Sources of water in England and Wales*

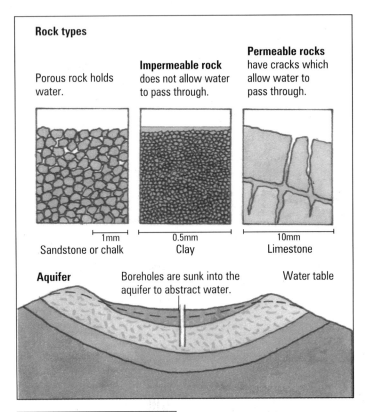

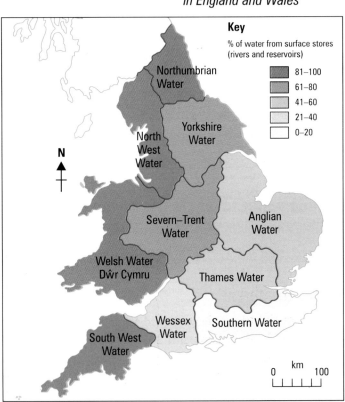

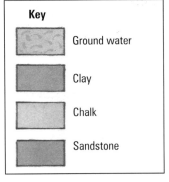

▲ **A** *How rocks affect where water is stored*

1 Using diagram A, copy and complete the following:
   Where water has seeped into the ground it can be stored in an .... Boreholes are .... into the aquifer to .... water.

2 Explain what the words **abstraction**, **porous**, and **impermeable** mean.

3 Using map B, list the parts of England and Wales that get:
   a) more than 60% of their water from water stored on the surface
   b) more than 60% of their water from the ground.

4 Describe the pattern shown on map B.

5 Using map B, suggest where in England and Wales you would expect most of the rocks to be impermeable.

Problems of over-abstraction

The level of the water in the ground is known as the water table. If the water table falls it means that water is being taken out faster than it is being replaced by rainfall seeping into the ground. This is known as over-abstraction.

Water company blamed for dried up river

The National Rivers Authority has told Thames Water to cut abstraction from the parched River Darent in Kent. This is one of a number of rivers in danger in the UK.

Thames Water said that the drought was the main reason for the river drying up. Four successive dry winters have meant insufficient rain seeping through the chalk hills around London to renew underground supplies. Demand for water has increased 70% in the last thirty years while in much of the south-east rainfall has fallen by 20% between 1988 and 1992. This increase has been met by abstracting more water from the aquifers causing the level of the water table to drop.

▲ **C** *Extract from* The Guardian, *16 June 1992*

Water treatment

It is essential to our health that water is clean before we drink it. Diagram E shows how water is treated to make it clean.

▲ **D** *The dried-up course of the River Darent in 1992*

6 Give two reasons why the River Darent dried up.

7 Why would each of the following people be concerned about over-abstraction:
   a) the manager of an industry that uses a lot of water
   b) someone interested in wildlife conservation
   c) the water company?

8 Use diagram E to explain:
   a) how treatment process removes particles of dirt
   b) how germs are killed.

9 *In April 1994, thousands of people in Worcester had their water cut off. Chemicals dissolved in the River Severn had polluted the drinking water. Explain why the treatment plant did not remove the chemicals.*

▼ **E** *Water treatment*

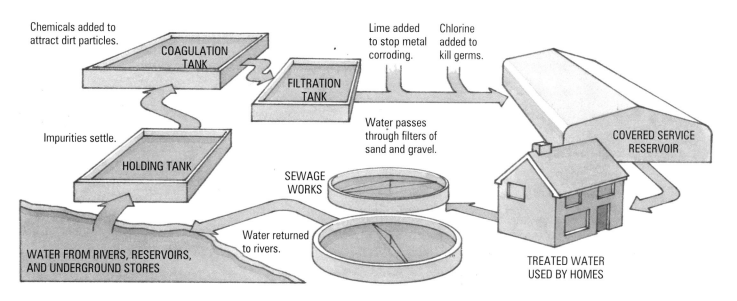

Water storage

Reservoirs are created to store water for later use. They are a way of providing a continual water supply when rainfall is variable. Carsington reservoir in the Severn-Trent Water region, the latest major reservoir to be built in the UK, was opened in May 1992.

Why was the Carsington reservoir needed?

Three million people live and work in Derbyshire, Leicestershire, and Nottinghamshire. In total they use 796 million litres of water every day. In a dry summer, homes and factories need even more water. As you can see from graph A, a new water supply was needed to meet this increased demand.

► **A** *Figures showed that in future there would not be enough water*

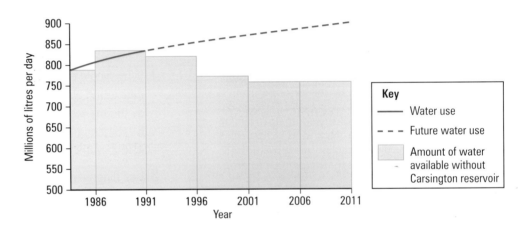

► **B** *Carsington reservoir*

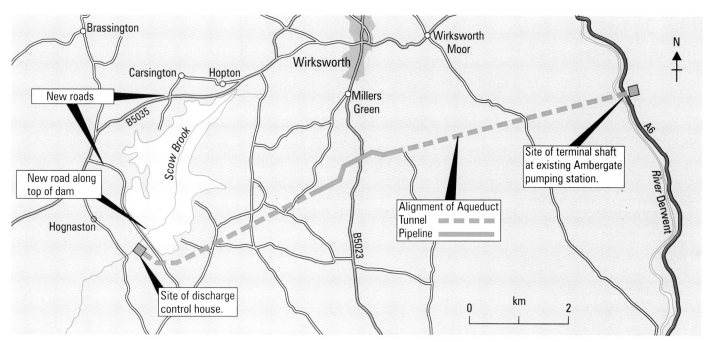

▲ **C** *Map of Carsington reservoir and the surrounding area*

How does the Carsington reservoir work?

No large rivers flow directly into the reservoir (as you can see from map C). During the winter, when the River Derwent is full of water, water is pumped along an aqueduct and into the reservoir. Then, when the river is low, or demand is high, water is pumped back into the river, ensuring ample water supplies from the river all year round.

The impact of building Carsington

In building the reservoir the landscape has obviously been changed; the land is now covered by water. This has had good and bad results. The area has lost farm land and buildings, but has gained a recreation site for water sports and other leisure activities.

Factfile: Carsington

- Two working farms were lost.
- Land from 30 other farms was lost – mostly medium to low quality farm land.
- Electricity lines had to be moved.
- One road was cut off by the reservoir.
- Jobs were created by the building and since then by the needs of visitors.
- There is increased traffic from visitors.
- The towns of Carsington and Hognaston were by-passed by new roads.

1 Use graph A.
  a) How much water will be used in the year 2011?
  b) How much water would be available in 2011 without Carsington?
  c) How much extra water is needed?

2 Use photo B and map C.
  a) How long is the aqueduct that takes water from the River Derwent to the reservoir and back?
  b) In what direction does water travel from the River Derwent to the reservoir?
  c) In what direction was the camera pointing to take photo B?

3 a) Discuss the good and bad effects of the reservoir.
  b) How might the following feel about the reservoir?
    (i) a local teenager
    (ii) a resident of Hopton
    (iii) a keen angler.
  c) Who do you think would benefit from the building of the reservoir? Who would lose out? Give reasons for your answer.

How do we manage this vital resource?

Water is a vital resource which must be managed carefully. The care of water in England and Wales is the responsibility of the National Rivers Authority (NRA). It is their job to:

● make sure that rivers and reservoirs do not dry up
● control water **pollution**, by taking action against people who pollute water
● provide protection from flooding.

▼ **A** *Different opinions on managing water resources*

Managing water resources

Could we use our existing water supplies more wisely instead of building new reservoirs? One way of doing this is to charge people according to the amount of water they use. This can be done using meters as we do for electricity and gas. The NRA would like to introduce meters in areas of water shortage. However, not everyone agrees that this is a good idea.

Meters stop people wasting water and prevent rivers from drying up.

My plants need regular watering. Why don't they reduce water wastage by fixing leaking mains pipes?

Since I've had a water meter, I can't afford to use the water we need. My four children have to use the same bath water, which is unhygienic.

We have a right to clean water. It is not a privilege that we should have to pay a lot for.

1 Make two <u>lists</u>, one with the arguments for water metering, the other with arguments against metering.

2 It has been suggested that more reservoirs could be built to solve water shortage problems, but there may be other solutions.

a) Discuss whether you think it would be better to build more reservoirs or try to conserve water by metering.

b) Write a letter addressed to the NRA saying what you think should be done.

▲ **B** *Common seal pups on the mud flats of the Tees estuary*

Managing pollution

Water quality has been improved in many rivers, by monitoring water quality and taking firm action against those responsible for pollution. In 1970 the **estuary** of the River Tees in north-east England was one of the most polluted in the UK. Today the Tees is much cleaner and wildlife is beginning to return, as photo B shows.

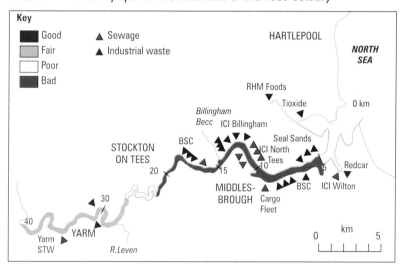

▲ **C** *Pollution levels in the River Tees in 1970*

▼ **D** *Pollution levels in the River Tees in 1990*

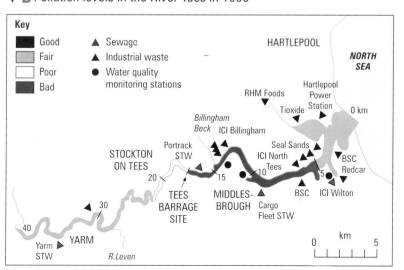

3 Describe the differences between maps C and D. Comment on:
- number of places where sewage and industrial waste enter the river
- quality of the river water (use the distances in km from the mouth to estimate the length of river affected by pollution).

Review

- Water covers 70% of the Earth but only 1% is available for us to use. Water is cleansed naturally in the water cycle, but many people still have to drink dirty water.
- Not all places receive the same amount of rainfall all through the year, and droughts cause problems for some farmers. Rain does not fall evenly in all places either, so water has to be stored, treated, and distributed to where it is needed.
- We must manage water carefully to ensure there is enough clean water for everyone.

4 Design a poster to make people think about the importance of water. Include some thought-provoking facts and figures, and an eyecatching map, graph, or diagram.

4 Tales of the river bank

Rivers are an important part of the landscape. They supply towns with water and carry away our waste. They can be used for transport, and for watersports such as canoeing and fishing. However, if they flood they can cause problems for the people living alongside them. In this unit we will find out what rivers are really like to live with, by asking:

- how do rivers shape the land?
- what are the causes and effects of river floods?
- how can flooding be controlled?

The course of the River Tees

Let's take a closer look at a river we heard about in the last unit, the River Tees. We will explore the river and the land around it as it flows off the high ground and down to the sea.

As the water flows down from Cross Fell it creates a **V-shaped valley**. This is a landform common in the upland section of rivers.

▼ **A** *The course of the River Tees*

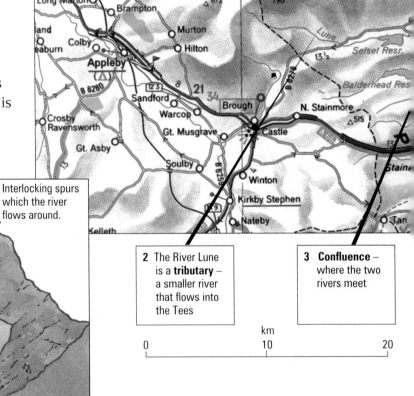

1 The **source** of a river is where it begins. The source of the Tees is in this upland area of Cumbria

2 The River Lune is a **tributary** – a smaller river that flows into the Tees

3 Confluence – where the two rivers meet

km

0   10   20

▼ **B** *V-shaped valley*

Weathering of the rocks produces loose material.

Loose material washed into river by rain.

Interlocking spurs which the river flows around.

Material carried by the river.

The river channel

The river erodes downwards and sideways.

◀ **C** *Estuary of the River Tees*

5 The **mouth** of the Tees, where it flows into the North Sea. On the Tees this section of the river is **tidal**. This means that salt water from the sea flows into the mouth of the river at high tide. This tidal section is known as an **estuary**.

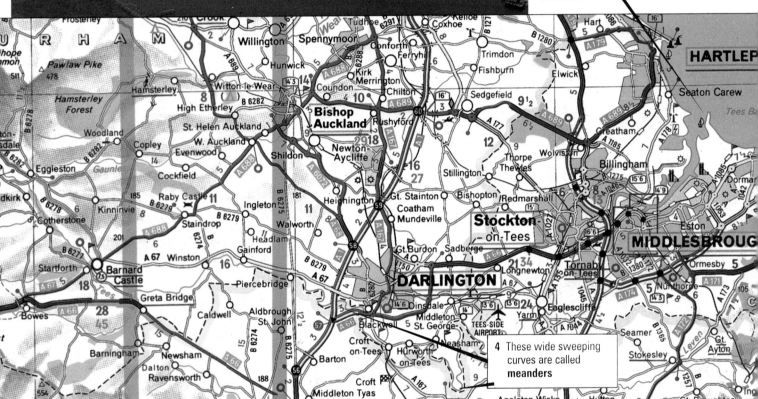

4 These wide sweeping curves are called **meanders**

1 Copy and complete the following passage, using map A.

The .... of the River Tees is in the high ground at Cross Fell which is .... metres above sea level. The Tees flows .... towards Barnard Castle. A total of .... tributaries, such as the Lune, join the Tees from the west before Barnard Castle. The Tees then flows .... towards Darlington, and on towards the city of .... which is on the tidal section of the river known as the ....

2 Use the scale line to work out the distance from the source to the mouth.

3 Use evidence from map A and photo C to suggest three ways the Tees is used by people.

4 How do the settlements (towns and villages) seem to change along the river? Suggest two reasons for your answer.

5 Using diagram B and photo C, describe the way in which the river and its valley have changed between the source and mouth.

The active river

Like all other rivers, the Tees is gradually shaping its own landscape.
- How does it do this?
- What kind of features does it create?

Changes in gradient

The course that the river follows is not always a smooth one. In the upland section of the river's course, the gradient may be steep, and sometimes vertical. The Tees drops suddenly like this at High Force, and the resulting waterfall is one of the most impressive land forms on the river.

How High Force Waterfall was formed

The Tees plunges down 27m at High Force. It falls over a ledge of very hard rock called whinstone (a local name for dolerite – an **igneous rock**). Beneath the whinstone is a layer of limestone, which is much more easily eroded. The force of the water cascading into the plunge pool, and the spray that it creates, erode the limestone at the base, leaving an overhang of whinstone above it. This is why you can sometimes stand behind a waterfall, at its base, without getting wet.

This overhang may collapse one day. As the waterfall continues to cut back it leaves a steep-sided gorge.

▶ **A** *High Force Waterfall*

1 Make a sketch of photo A and label it using the following words:
Plunge pool
Waterfall
Steep-sided valley (gorge)
River Tees

▶ **B** *Cross-section through High Force Waterfall*

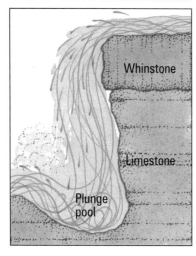

Whinstone

Limestone

Plunge pool

The lowland section of the Tees

The landscape in the lower section of the river, shown in photo D, is quite different from the V-shaped valleys and waterfalls of the upland section. Look at the map of the River Tees on page 37, and find the town of Yarm. Can you see the many wide sweeping curves? These are **meanders**.

Meanders

Have you ever been on a waterslide? If you have, you will know that your weight throws you against the outside of the bend. A similar thing happens to the water in the river. As it travels round a meander the fastest flow is on the outside of the bend. The force of this fast-moving water, and any sediment that it is carrying, is enough to **erode** the river bank, creating a river cliff. The water on the inside of the meander, however, moves much more slowly. It no longer has enough energy to carry the **sediment** it is holding, so this material is **deposited**, forming a river beach.

► C

The features of a meander

River cliff on outside bend

Direction of flow

River beach on inside bend

▼ D *Aerial view of Yarm*

2 Compare photos A and D by completing a table like this:

	High Force	Yarm
River width		
Gradient of river		
Land use next to river		

3 Look at photo D, of Yarm. Describe the land on the sides of the river. What problem might the river cause here?

4 Draw a labelled sketch of the river in photo C. Predict what will happen if the eroding and depositing of material continues and try to show this on your sketch.

The gift of the Nile

Our need for water as a resource has meant that, all over the world, settlements have grown up close to rivers. Yarm and Middlesbrough are examples, on the River Tees. This strong connection between rivers and settlements is particularly noticeable along the banks of the River Nile, one of the longest rivers in the world. The valley and delta of the River Nile is only 4% of Egypt's land area, but 99% of Egypt's population live there.

▶ **A** *Course of the River Nile from source to mouth*

Using the River Nile

About 90% of Egypt is desert but there is a narrow strip (or corridor) of farm land on either side of the river. For many years, water from the Nile has been used to irrigate this corridor.

▼ **B** *Oxen are used to turn a wheel which draws fresh water from a well*

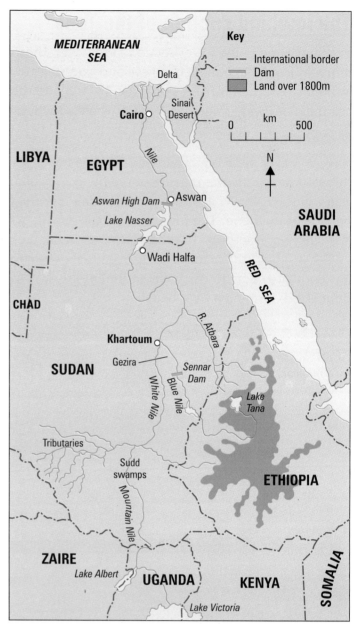

1 a) In which country is the source of the Blue Nile?
  b) What city is at the confluence of the two main tributaries of the Nile?
  c) Which sea does the Nile flow into?

2 Use photo B to describe:
  a) the landscape in the background
  b) how the oxen are used
  c) how the buildings are designed to keep the inside cool (page 19 will help).

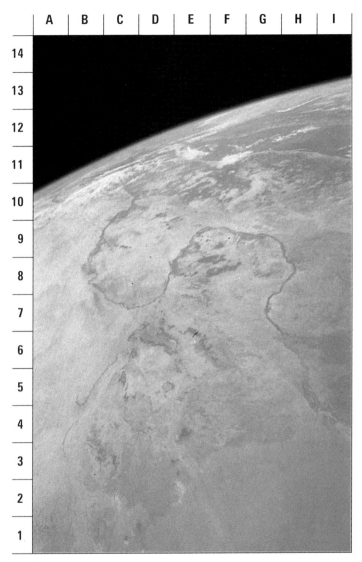

▲ **C** *Satellite image showing the River Nile meandering across Sudan, with Egypt in the distance*

Controlling the flow in Egypt

In the past, an annual flood covered the fields on either side of the Nile in a layer of fertile silt, but the floods no longer happen. The Aswan High Dam holds back the flood water, and releases it slowly in the drier months. Not only does this prevent flooding, which often caused the loss of life and property, but it also generates electricity. The dam also traps silt, so farmers have to buy fertilizer to improve the soil. This is expensive for the smaller farmers.

Controlling the flow in Sudan

Just as in Egypt, most people in Sudan live close to the Nile. The area of Gezira lies between the two main tributaries of the Nile, south of Khartoum. You can see this darker area on satellite image C in grid square I6. It has always benefited from the water and the rich soil deposited by the Nile. Two dams on the Blue Nile supply the area with irrigation water. Gezira is now an oasis of farm land covering $900 \, km^2$, and employing over 220 000 farmers and labourers. The small farms (6–8 hectares) are rented from the government. Gezira produces 70% of Sudan's cotton, and 50% of the country's wheat. The cotton is exported and earns 30% of the country's wealth.

3 Match the following list of features which can be seen on satellite image C, to the correct grid reference:

Red Sea   Nile delta   D11   E12
Gezira   Sinai desert   I6   H12

4 Use the following headings to make notes on the benefits of controlling the Nile:

The effect on farming
The benefits for people living close to the Nile
The benefits for towns, cities, and industries

5 Make a tracing or sketch of map A.
   a) Mark on it where most people live in Egypt and Sudan.
   b) Compare your map to map F on page 29. Which country has the most uneven population distribution?
   c) Explain why the patterns are so different.

6 *How might the Egyptians feel if the Sudanese government built more dams on the Nile? Describe the effects this might have on Egypt.*

A tale of two floods

Living close to a river can be risky. When streets and homes are flooded by rivers, we might well ask:
- why is it flooding here, and why now?
- why do some floods cause more damage than others?

French floods

One man lost his business, others lost cars, others had their vineyards destroyed. Everyone lost something.

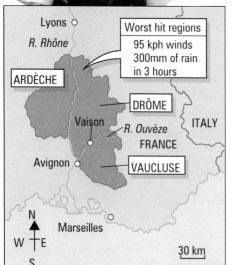

Floods kill 32 in violent French storms

At least 32 people were killed and 44 missing after violent storms and flash floods swept the Ardèche, Vaucluse and Drôme regions in S.E. France. Four helicopters were used to rescue at least 100 people hanging onto debris or sitting on roofs as 95 kph winds made the use of small boats almost impossible.

The worst hit area was the small town of Vaison la Romaine where houses were demolished by a wall of water. Vehicles were carried away and in some cases their passengers were drowned. Falling trees crushed cars and houses. Many of the country roads were blocked by landslides, mud and broken bridges.

Weather experts said that although heavy rain was common, the latest storms were exceptional. About 40% of the region's annual rainfall had fallen in a matter of hours.

▲ **A** *Extract from* The Guardian, *24 September 1992*

▲ **B** *People salvaging the remains of their property in Vaison la Romaine*

◀ **C** *The area affected by flooding*

1 Use extract A and photo B.
  a) List the damage done by the storms and flooding.
  b) Why were people in cars at risk, and what weather conditions made the rescue operation difficult?

2 Copy and complete the following, using map C.
  The Rhône flows in a .... direction through .... The region worst hit by the storms and flooding was .... km across from west to east and .... km from north to south. The town of Vaison la Romaine is built on the Ouvèze which is a .... of the Rhône.

Map labels: Lyons, R. Rhône, ARDÈCHE, Worst hit regions — 95 kph winds, 300mm of rain in 3 hours, DRÔME, Vaison, R. Ouvèze, FRANCE, ITALY, Avignon, VAUCLUSE, Marseilles, N W E S, 30 km

Flooding in the USA

In June 1993 the River Mississippi burst its banks, covering an area the size of England with water. The floods killed 45 people, drove 30 000 people from their homes, and caused US $10 billion worth of damage. Heavy rain was the main cause of the floods. The course of the Mississippi has been artificially straightened, to move flood water downstream quickly. This may have made the floods downstream even worse.

3 a) Make a simple tracing or copy of map E to show the outline of the Mississippi drainage basin.

b) Mark on the map the areas worst hit by flooding, which included:

Minnesota Wisconsin South Dakota Nebraska
Iowa Kansas Missouri Illinois

4 What are the similarities and differences between the floods in France and the USA? Consider:

Size Damage Causes

▲ **D**
The Mississippi River flooding its banks

5 Imagine you are a news reporter at one of the floods. Describe the scene in a report. Include the views of residents, business people, and emergency services.

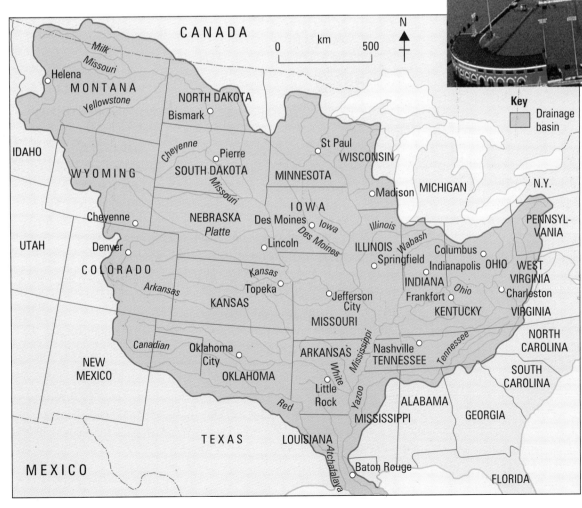

◄ **E**
The Mississippi River and its drainage basin

How can the risk of flooding be reduced ?

1 Using dams to control the flow

Dams can be built across a river to hold back water at times of peak flow. Many of the world's rivers have been controlled in this way, for example the Aswan High Dam on the River Nile (see pages 40–41), and the Glen Canyon Dam on the River Colorado (page 85). These large dams are very expensive to build, but once they are built they generate cheap **hydro-electric power** (HEP).

2 Straightening the river

Straightening the river makes the river's water flow more quickly. Flood water quickly passes the danger point. Straightening the river also makes it quicker and easier for boats to travel up and down. Some of the bends on the River Tees were straightened for this reason.

▲ **B** *Trying to prevent flood damage during the Mississippi floods, June 1993*

▼ **A** *How people have changed the Mississippi*

1932
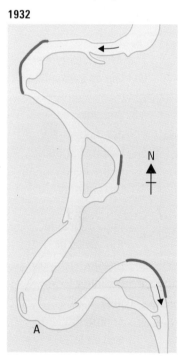

1941
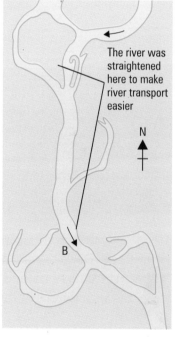

The river was straightened here to make river transport easier

1975
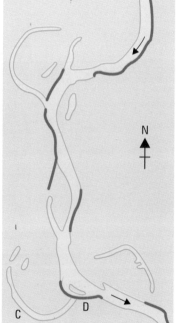

1 Study diagram A, then:
a) describe the river feature at A
b) explain what has happened at B
c) describe and explain how the feature A has changed to C.
d) Why do you think people have had to strengthen the bank at D?
Page 39 will help you check your answers to these questions.

Key
—— Where the bank has been strengthened with steel or concrete

3 Keeping the water in

By building **embankments** along each side of the river, the banks are artificially raised. The River Mississippi has 4000km of these along its course. In China, embankments have been built along both banks of the Lower Yellow River for 1400km. These embankments are 10m high.

In February 1995, in the low flat land of the Netherlands, embankments held back the flood waters of the rivers Waal and Maas. If they had broken, towns and villages would have been under four or five metres of water. 250 000 people fled their homes as the levels of the rivers rose. The embankments, known as dykes, have an outer skin of clay and an inner core of sand. In places the clay was eroded and water began to seep through. People worked through the night reinforcing the dykes with sand bags and sheets of polythene. Map C shows the affected area.

▼ **C** *Area threatened by floods in the Netherlands, February 1995*

2 Sketch photo D. Label the river, flood plain, embankments, and irrigated fields.

3 Write about the advantages and disadvantages of each flood protection method (dams, river straightening, embankments). Use the following headings to help you:

Impact on the flooding   Impact on people   Cost

4 What factors would a government have to consider before it chose which flood protection measure to adopt?

◀ **D** *Rebuilding a flood embankment in China*

Review

Rivers are an important part of our landscape. They shape the land in different ways.
- V-shaped valleys and waterfalls are common in the upland section.
- Meanders are common in the lowland section. Rivers can cause widespread damage when they flood. Despite this, many people live close to rivers. We have tried to reduce the risk of flooding with different degrees of success.

5 If you have a river nearby, why not investigate it? Find out where its source is and where it goes to. Discover whether it ever floods, and who this affects.

5 Bangladesh

Bangladesh is a country in south Asia. In studying this developing country we will review some ideas from the earlier units:
- **what are the landscape and climate of Bangladesh like?**
- **how do the great rivers that flow across Bangladesh affect the people who live there?**
- **how is this country linked to the rest of the world?**

BANGLADESH

Bangladesh is a lush, green country. Most of it is formed by the **delta** of the River Ganges, the largest delta in the world. Bangladesh is home to exotic animals such as the Bengal tiger, black bear, gecko lizard, and many poisonous snakes. It has over 500 species of bird including the mynah and the fishing eagle. Most of the land is flat and low-lying. But there are hills in the north-east that rise to 240 metres and in the south-east to 600 metres.

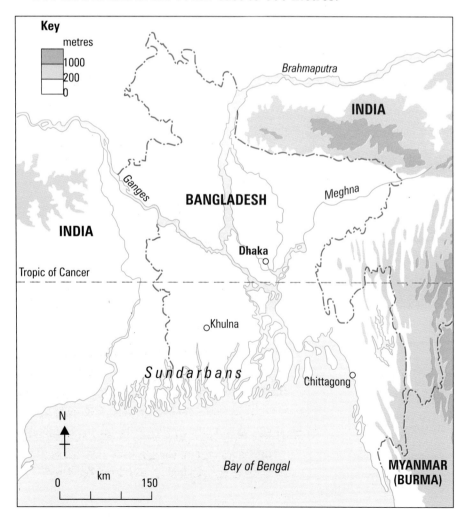

◀ **A** *Bangladesh in south Asia*

Key

metres
1000
200
0

Brahmaputra

INDIA

Ganges

BANGLADESH

Meghna

INDIA

Dhaka

Tropic of Cancer

Khulna

S u n d a r b a n s

Chittagong

N

Bay of Bengal

MYANMAR (BURMA)

km
0   150

Factfile: Bangladesh

- Population: 122 280 000
- The capital city is Dhaka (Dacca), population 6 105 000.
- The other big cities are Chittagong (pop 2 041 000) and Khulna (pop 877 000).
- **The Gross National Product** (GNP) is US $220 per person.
- The main exports are jute (33%), fish (12%), skins and hides (12%).
- The farm land is very fertile, and can grow two or three crops a year.

How the landscape is formed

Bangladesh has been formed from the sediment deposited by the River Ganges (Padma), River Brahmaputra (Jumana), and the River Meghna. These rivers start in the Himalaya mountains. As they flow through Bangladesh they split up into a giant delta. In the delta, the water deposits its sediment as diagram B shows, forming new land.

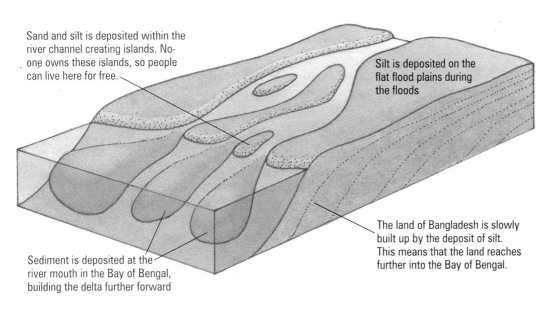

Sand and silt is deposited within the river channel creating islands. No-one owns these islands, so people can live here for free.

Silt is deposited on the flat flood plains during the floods

Sediment is deposited at the river mouth in the Bay of Bengal, building the delta further forward

The land of Bangladesh is slowly built up by the deposit of silt. This means that the land reaches further into the Bay of Bengal.

◄ **B** *How the delta was formed*

◄ **C** *Mouth of the Ganges. In the delta areas some people live on houseboats. They travel along the rivers to trade with rural communities*

1 Find Bangladesh on map A.
  a) Which country almost surrounds Bangladesh?
  b) Which other country shares a border with Bangladesh?
  c) In what direction, and how far, is Chittagong from Dhaka?

2 Draw a map of Bangladesh, showing Dhaka, Chittagong, the Bay of Bengal and the Rivers Ganges, Brahmaputra, and Meghna. Shade the map to show low flat ground, and high ground, and label them.

3 a) Use diagram B to explain in your own words how the landscape of Bangladesh was formed.
  b) Why is Bangladesh at risk from flooding?

Contrasts between city and rural life

- What is it like to live in the countryside in Bangladesh?
- How different is life in the city?

Rural life in the Khulna region

Two-thirds of Khulna is marshland or dense jungle and an absolute haven for wildlife. In the south are the Sundarbans ('beautiful forest'), a huge, almost untouched, waterlogged jungle. The Sundarbans are the largest mangrove belt in the world, stretching 80km in from the coast. They cover an area of 38500km^2, of which about one third is covered in water.

There are no permanent settlements within the forest apart from a few government workforce camps for the extraction of timber. These camps are all either built on stilts or they 'hang' from the trees, because of the soft ground. The ground is all bog down to a depth of 2 metres.

▲ **A** *Extract from* Bangladesh, a Travel Survival Kit

The wildlife reserves in the Sundarbans are a success. It is estimated that there are 400 Bengal tigers in the Sundarbans. Hunting is banned and the number of tigers is increasing. But the forest is also a huge resource for people on the edge of the forest who need its trees for firewood and shipbuilding. The people fish in the rivers, and gather honey and plants from the forest.

Farming in Bangladesh

Farm land in Bangladesh is very fertile because of the silt deposited by the great rivers that cross the country. While 57% of the population work on the land, most of the farm land is owned by a small number of rich, powerful people. Most farmers own only a small plot of land, or none at all. The average size of a family farm is 50m × 100m (half a **hectare**).

For the poor farmer or landless labourer, life in the countryside is hard; 40% of farmers do not have farm animals or even a plough. The land is often flooded by the great rivers and by the sea. Flooding might destroy all the crops of a small farmer, as well as the family home.

1 Copy the following sentences that you think are true, and correct the others as you rewrite them.
   a) The Sundarbans are a wildlife reserve.
   b) The Sundarbans are covered in tropical rainforest. Many people live there.
   c) All the farms in Bangladesh are large, and the soil is poor.

2 In what way is the forest of the Sundarbans a resource?

3 Discuss how farms could be improved. Suggest the improvements you would make.

▼ **B** *A small family farm plot*

City life

Only 14% of the people in Bangladesh live in towns or cities, and most of these live in the main cities of Dhaka, Chittagong, and Khulna (see factfile on page 46). Central Dhaka looks like many other large city centres with tall, modern buildings. Some of the people who live here are quite well off. But most people in the cities are poor, although they earn two or three times more money than in the country. Many of them live in **squatter settlements**, like those in photo C. They live there because they cannot afford to live anywhere else and the government cannot provide houses either cheaply or quickly enough. The number of people in the cities is growing rapidly. The population of Dhaka is expected to reach 11.2 million by the year 2000.

4 Look at photo D. List the forms of transport used in the city.

5 Describe the scene in photo C. Think about
a) where the settlement is **b)** where the people cook
c) where they get their water.

6 Imagine you have just moved to Dhaka from a small family farm. Write a letter home describing what you think about the city. Would you advise your friend to move, too?

▲ **C** *Squatter settlements*

◄ **D** *A busy street in Dhaka. Many people are pedalled about in rickshaws or driven in autorickshaws*

The flood problem

Flooding happens every year in Bangladesh. Sometimes the flooding is very severe. In 1988, 80% of the land was under water, over 3000 people died, and about 3 million were made homeless.
● Why does Bangladesh have floods?
● What are the effects of the flooding?
Bangladesh has three large rivers running through it. The low-lying **flood plains** of these rivers become covered in flood water when there is too much rainfall.

Two main causes of the flooding

Heavy rainfall every year during June, July, and August causes the rivers to swell so much that they burst their banks and flood the surrounding land. These seasonal rains are called the **monsoon**. **Tropical cyclones** also cause flooding. Violent storms in the Bay of Bengal push sea water inland, covering coastal areas with sea water.

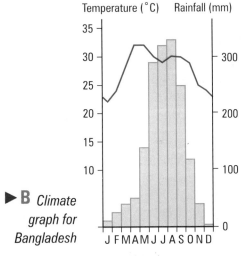

▶ **B** *Climate graph for Bangladesh*

▼ **A** *The rivers and annual rainfall of Bangladesh, India, and Nepal*

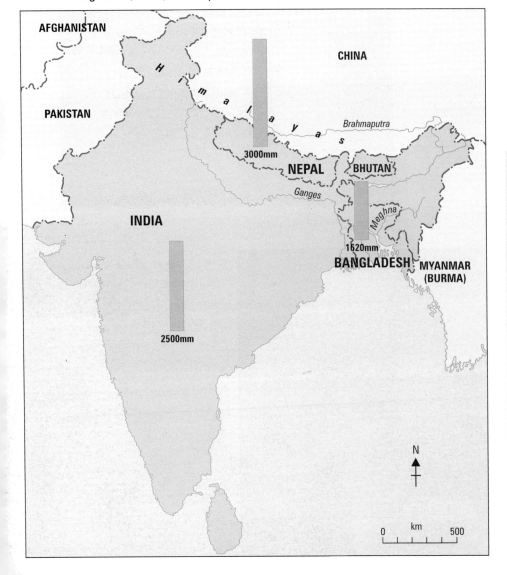

1 Look at graph B.
  a) In which month does the monsoon start?
  b) In which month is rainfall highest?
  c) How long does the monsoon last?

2 a) Which country on map A has most rainfall?
  b) Why is the flooding an international problem?

3 Southern Sudan also has a seasonal rainfall pattern, as you can see on page 28. Copy out the statements below that you think are true, and correct the others as you rewrite them.
  a) The rainy season in both countries lasts from April to October.
  b) Sudan has nearly four times more rain in July than Bangladesh.
  c) Both countries have similar amounts of rainfall in the winter months.

The results of the flooding

Flooding in Bangladesh always has some bad effects. Homes are destroyed, food is lost, and people drown. The sea water is particularly bad for the farm land, leaving salt which kills the crops. When the flooding starts, people move to higher ground where they will be safe. They have to leave everything behind.

Immediate and long term effects

Drowning and the loss of property are the immediate effects of the flooding. But flooding brings about many other problems, and some of these last long after the flood waters have gone down. Roads and railways may have been swept away, and may take weeks to repair and make safe. People may fall ill, or suffer because they can't get enough to eat during the weeks after the flood. People also may suffer from **dehydration** (lack of water) because water supplies become contaminated.

Is it all bad news?

River flooding does have some good effects.
- Every year the flooding rivers deposit fertile silt on the farm land. This enables the people to grow up to three crops of rice a year.
- The floods renew fish stocks in the lakes and ponds.
- The flood waters from the rivers refill wells and ground water supplies.

4 Look at photos C, D, and the one on the cover. Describe the problems caused by the flooding in each photo. Which of these would be long term problems?

5 Discuss in groups why diseases like cholera and dysentery might occur as a result of the flooding.

6 *Why might the long term effects of flooding be of greater concern in Bangladesh than in the USA?*

▼ **C** *Flooding in Dhaka*

▼ **D** *Cyclone damage at the airport in Chittagong*

Can the flooding be controlled?

We saw on pages 44–45 that flooding can be controlled, and that each method has its advantages and disadvantages. What would be the best plan for Bangladesh?

The Flood Action Plan (FAP)

The World Bank has suggested that Bangladesh's flood problem could be solved by a huge scheme called the Flood Action Plan (FAP). Diagram A explains the scheme.

1 Use map A on page 46 to name the features labelled A to C on diagram A.

▼ **A** *Proposed Flood Action Plan for Bangladesh*

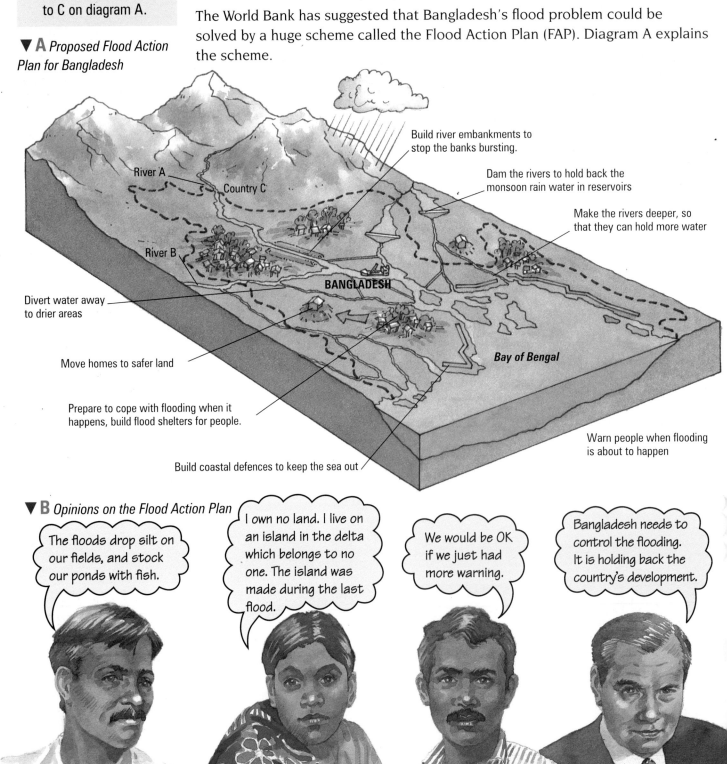

Build river embankments to stop the banks bursting.

Dam the rivers to hold back the monsoon rain water in reservoirs

Make the rivers deeper, so that they can hold more water

River A

Country C

River B

BANGLADESH

Divert water away to drier areas

Move homes to safer land

Bay of Bengal

Prepare to cope with flooding when it happens, build flood shelters for people.

Build coastal defences to keep the sea out

Warn people when flooding is about to happen

▼ **B** *Opinions on the Flood Action Plan*

The floods drop silt on our fields, and stock our ponds with fish.

I own no land. I live on an island in the delta which belongs to no one. The island was made during the last flood.

We would be OK if we just had more warning.

Bangladesh needs to control the flooding. It is holding back the country's development.

▲ **C** *Some flood embankments have already been constructed*

Is the FAP the best solution?

Some experts believe that the FAP is a mistake. They believe that the FAP will:
- cost billions of dollars
- take years to construct
- require constant maintenance
- need the co-operation of the surrounding countries.

Also, many believe that embankments on the River Mississippi in the USA (page 43) may have made recent flooding worse, not better.

Are there any alternatives?

There are alternatives to the FAP that would be less expensive, and therefore may be more appropriate to Bangladesh. For example, they could:
- provide better prediction and warnings of floods
- build flood shelters for people, their possessions and livestock
- prepare emergency services for quick and effective help after a flood.

These flood controls are too expensive. We will have to borrow money from abroad.

You can never control floods, you can only try to reduce the risk to lives and property.

Damage caused by flooding costs millions. It must be controlled.

2 a) List the reasons for the FAP.
   b) List the arguments against the FAP.

3 Working in pairs or small groups, write a report on Bangladesh's flood problem and the FAP for a radio broadcast. Include in your report:
   a) a brief description of the problem
   b) an outline of the proposals
   c) the reasons why some people oppose the scheme. Make sure your report is punchy and interesting and can be read in no more than 45 seconds!

The Bangladeshi community in the UK

In the 1950s, when the UK was short of workers, the British government advertised jobs to people living in countries of the former British Empire. Many people moved to the UK, mainly from the countries of the Caribbean or southern Asia, to find work and a new home.

Mr Khan's story

Mr Khan (photo A) lives in Tower Hamlets, London. He was born in 1930 in Bangladesh. During his childhood in Bangladesh he learnt to speak English, and was taught British history in school. When he grew up he travelled to the UK. He wanted to learn better English, to see the country he had heard so much about and earn money for his family.

▼ **A** *Mr Khan of Tower Hamlets*

▲ **B** *Grocers in Tower Hamlets*

Mr Khan moved from Sylhet in Bangladesh to the UK in 1958 and his first jobs were unskilled and low paid. He earned £5 a week working in a chemical factory in Kent. He managed to send about £1 a week back to his parents and brothers in Bangladesh. In 1966 he moved to London and worked for a tailor. He opened his own tailoring business in 1971. Later he opened a grocery and a Bangladeshi restaurant.

▼ C *East London Mosque, Tower Hamlets*

Mr Khan has settled in London and now has three children and seven grandchildren living there. He is one of a community of 50 000 Bangladeshi people in Tower Hamlets. In all there are 200 000 Bangladeshi people living in the UK. Like Mr Khan, these people have strong links with Bangladesh. They go there to see friends and relatives, they import foods like fish, vegetables, and rice to sell to the Bangladeshi people in the UK. Many Bangladeshis working in the UK and other countries send money back to their relatives in Bangladesh. This money is important to the economy of Bangladesh.

▼ D *How family income is spent in Bangladesh and UK*

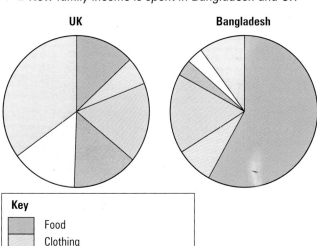

UK   **Bangladesh**

Key
- Food
- Clothing
- Energy and housing
- Medicine and education
- Transport
- Other (eg TV, electrical goods, holidays, savings, luxuries)

Key
Number of Bangladeshi people
- 50000–100000
- 20000–50000
- 10000–20000
- 5000–10000
- 2000–5000
- Less than 2000

N

km
0   100

▲ E *The Bangladeshi communities in the UK*

1 Why did Mr Khan move to the UK?

2 Try to imagine yourself as Mr Khan in 1958. Draw up a table like the one below, and use the information on this page and page 49 to fill it in.

	Stay in Bangladesh	Move to the UK
Advantages		
Disadvantages		

3 Do you think Mr Khan made a good decision? Why?

4 Look at photos A, B and C.
   a) What links do you think the Bangladeshi people in Tower Hamlets have with Bangladesh?
   b) Suggest some reasons why they want to keep these links.

5 Using map E describe where, apart from London, the main Bangladeshi communities are in the UK.

6 Look at the pie charts in D.
   a) How much of their income does the average family in Bangladesh and the UK spend on food?
   b) Describe and explain the other differences you can see between the two pie charts.

How does Bangladesh compare?

We have seen in this unit that Bangladesh is similar to other countries. Its climate, for example, is similar to other parts of south and south-east Asia. It is easily flooded, a problem shared by other places we have studied (for example, parts of France and the USA). It also has strong community links, as we have seen, with the UK.

So how does Bangladesh compare with the UK? The first comparisons are very easy. The climate and landscapes are very different. Also Bangladesh is one of the poorest countries in the world and the UK is one of the richest.

Data about
▼ **A** *the UK and Bangladesh*

Measure	UK	Bangladesh
Population (millions)	58.0	122.3
GNP (US $ per person)	16 750	220
Number of births per 1000 people	14	41
Number of deaths per 1000 people	12	14
Life expectancy (male/female)	73/79	53/53
Population per doctor	300	6500
% urban population	93	14

1 Using table A, which country:
  a) is wealthier?
  b) has a lower birth rate?
  c) has a bigger rural population?

2 Table A shows that people in the UK can expect to live longer than people in Bangladesh. Suggest some reasons for this. Think about health care, diet, and the way of life.

3 Use the pie charts in B to describe what has happened to:
  a) the population of the whole country
  b) the percentage of people living in towns and cities
  c) the total number of people living in towns and cities.

4 What can you suggest to explain the growth of towns and cities in Bangladesh?

The growing population of Bangladesh

The information in diagram B shows that the population is growing rapidly, and that only 14% of people in Bangladesh live in urban areas (towns or cities). In Dhaka, the capital, 50% of the people live in slums or squatter settlements, and only half of the proper homes have tapped water. No houses in the countryside have tapped water; it comes either from wells, ponds, or rivers.

Key
Population growth
Urban population growth

▼ **B** *Bangladesh: population growth and the percentage of urban population*

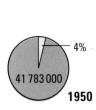

41 783 000 — 4%
1950

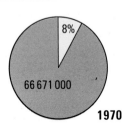

66 671 000 — 8%
1970

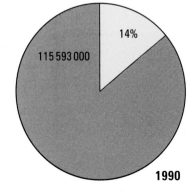

115 593 000 — 14%
1990

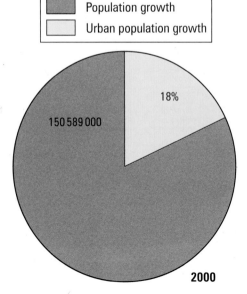

150 589 000 — 18%
2000

The youthful population of Bangladesh

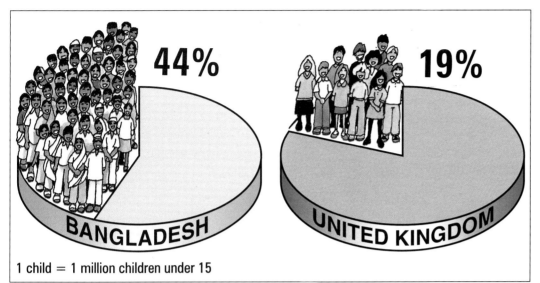

44% BANGLADESH
19% UNITED KINGDOM

1 child = 1 million children under 15

◀ **C** *The proportion of children in UK and Bangladesh populations*

▼ **D** *Opinions from government and children in Bangladesh and the UK*

Our Government spends 2.2% of GNP on schools

I will leave school when I am ten

I may leave school at sixteen and go to college

Our Government spends 4.7% of GNP on schools

35% of people in our country can read and write

99% of people in our country can read and write

5 Use diagram C.
  a) What proportion of the population in Bangladesh is under 15?
  b) In what way is the population of the two countries different?

6 What do you think a Bangladeshi child will do after leaving school at 10?

7 Use one piece of information from table A to draw a graph which compares the two countries. The style of diagrams B and C may give you an idea about the best way to show the information.

Review

Bangladesh is a developing country. Most people live in rural areas and work on small farms. It is a densely populated and fertile country. Several great rivers cross the flat landscape, and there have been a number of destructive floods. The government must now decide how to deal with the flood threat.

6 Rural communities in the UK

In this unit we will be investigating:
- **what it is like to live in a rural area**
- **how settlements and jobs are changing in the countryside**
- **how these changes affect the landscape.**

Why is the countryside important?

Most people in the UK (93%) live in **urban areas**, that is in towns and cities. However, the UK is small, and nowhere is very far from the countryside. Whether we live there or not, the countryside is important to us. It produces much of our food, and resources such as stone and timber. It contains a variety of landscapes and habitats, and it is somewhere many of us like to spend our leisure time. But the rural environment is changing quickly, as we shall see.

Rural change

Increased use of machinery, fertilizers, and pesticides on UK farms over the last 50 years has resulted in a number of major changes in the countryside. These changes have affected the people who live in **rural areas**, and the landscape too, as flow diagram B shows.

▼ **A** *Satellite image of south-east England. The yellow colour is from fields of oilseed rape. This is a crop which has been introduced to England recently because of a subsidy (money given to farmers) from the European Union*

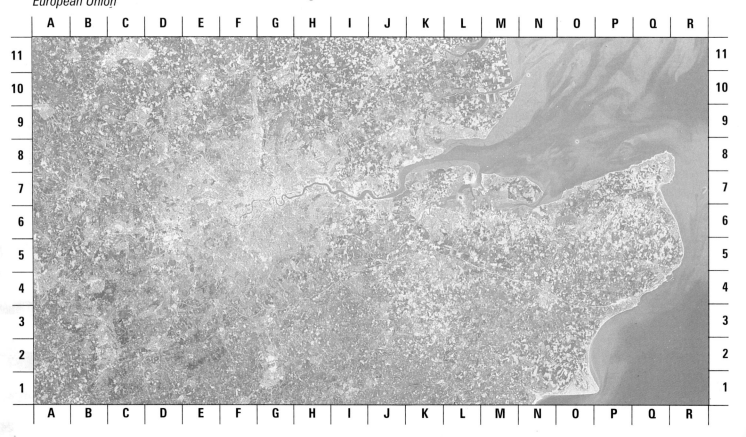

► **B** *Flow diagram, rural change*

Tractors and fertilizers used on UK farms

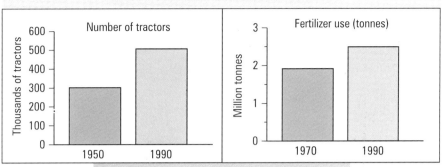

Mechanization of farms has led to

Job losses and bigger farms

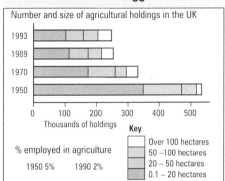

Number and size of agricultural holdings in the UK

% employed in agriculture
1950 5%   1990 2%

Key
Over 100 hectares
50 –100 hectares
20 – 50 hectares
0.1 – 20 hectares

Increased food production

Loss of natural habitats and wildlife

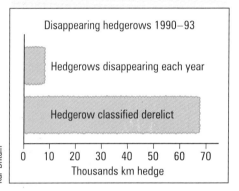

Because we now produce too much food in Europe, the European Union (EU) is reducing subsidies to some farmers. This has led farmers to look for alternative sources of income

1 Using image A, match the list below to the correct grid reference.

Estuary of the River Thames	G7
Mainly fields of oilseed rape	N9
A group of reservoirs	N8
Large meander	L8
Shallow water	P6
Deeper water	D5

2 Describe how the number of tractors on UK farms has changed.

3 a) How many farms in total were there in 1950 and 1993?
b) How many farms under 20 hectares were there in 1950 and 1993?
c) Why has mechanization and the increase in farm size led to job losses?

4 How much hedgerow is lost each year? Why do you think mechanization led to the loss of hedgerows?

This farmer has a drinks machine in his farmyard for walkers

5 *In what ways could farmers use their land in the future? Can you suggest any land uses that will create new jobs?*

6 *Why should we preserve hedgerows? Think about the benefits to wildlife and the farmer.*

Communities in the countryside

Many people who live and work in the countryside live in small **settlements**, similar to those shown on this and the next page.

- What kinds of settlements are there in rural areas?
- What kind of facilities do they have?

▼ **A** *Aerial view of Rushbury*

The village community

Rushbury and Munslow lie to the north and south of Wenlock Edge, a limestone escarpment (a long, low hill) in south Shropshire. Both are old farming settlements. The people who live in this rural area have very few local facilities. Munslow has a Post Office, a pub, and a garage. But it has no other shops, no school, and the doctor only comes to the surgery one day a week. It used to have a butcher, a baker, a grocer and a small primary school, but these have all closed over the last few years.

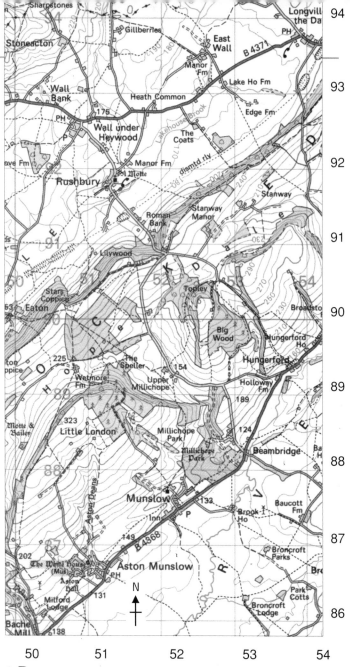

▲ **B** *Rushbury and Munslow at 1:50 000*

1 a) Estimate the number of houses in Rushbury.

b) The average household size in south Shropshire is 2.4. How many people might live in Rushbury?

2 Using photo A and map B, find any evidence that Rushbury is:

a) a very old settlement

b) still an active farming community.

3 Decide in which direction the camera was pointing to take the aerial photo of Rushbury:

north   south-west

north-east   another

4 What is the river feature in map B at 5286?

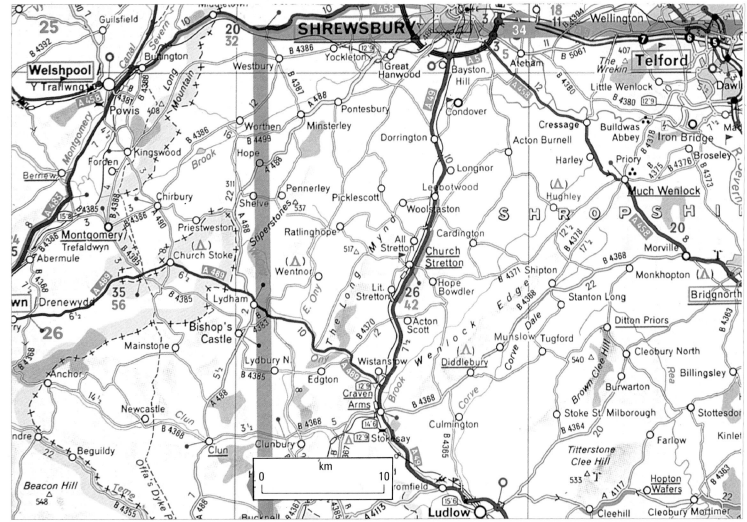

▲ C Bishop's Castle and the surrounding area, from a road atlas

Village life

Fred, 67, has just walked five miles to the inn and back home again. He does this most Thursdays, so that he can collect two loaves of bread.

He made the arrangement about the bread with Vic, the landlord, after the last shop in Munslow closed two years ago. It saves a trip to Ludlow, the local town. He walks because he doesn't own a car, and these days the bus only goes twice a week. Fred is not on the telephone.

▲ D Extract adapted from The Observer, 24 March 1994

> We live close to Rushbury. We chose to live here because it's so beautiful and quiet. It's nice to be able to walk on Wenlock Edge. We both commute: I work in Shrewsbury and Brian works in Church Stretton.

▲ E Kate Campion

5 Use road map C to find out how far the children of Munslow have to go to:
a) primary school (Diddlebury)
b) secondary school (Ludlow)
c) sixth form college (Ludlow or Shrewsbury).

6 a) What seem to be the advantages and disadvantages of living in a village?
b) Why is rural life easier for Kate than for Fred?

7 Why do you think so many village shops in places like Munslow have closed down in recent years?

▲ **A** *Aerial view of Bishop's Castle*

A larger rural community

Bishop's Castle, close to the Welsh border, was planned as a new town in the 12th century. The main street runs from the church at the bottom of the hill, to the castle site at the top. The town is small, but it has a number of shops and services, as you can see in the factfile. The shops, the college, and the market all serve the needs of people who live in the surrounding rural area. The area that a settlement serves is called its **catchment area**.

> **Factfile: Bishop's Castle**
>
> - Population: 1569.
> - The town has:
> - a weekly livestock market
> - 41 different shops and offices
> - a primary school (150 pupils)
> - a school for 11–18 year-olds, the Community College (500 pupils).
>   The College has a catchment area of 500km^2 (population 9080; population density 18 people per km^2).

1 Using photo A, match the features in the list below to the correct grid reference:

Castle mound	B12	College	F15
Church	C16	Cattle market	D6

▶ **B** *Bishop's Castle High Street*

Stuck in the middle of the country

The town has enough shops for everyday needs such as groceries. However, the shops don't have much variety, and they don't stock many different brands. There are no specialist shops; there is nowhere to buy the latest fashions, CDs, furniture, hi-fi, or videos. People have to go elsewhere for these things. As diagram D shows, 70% of the locals regularly go shopping in one of the bigger towns nearby. They are attracted to the large supermarkets there.

Bishop's Castle is in an isolated location. Having to travel a long way to do the shopping is just one problem. It takes well over twenty minutes for ambulances to reach Bishop's Castle from their station near Ludlow. The ambulance would then take you to Shrewsbury hospital, another 35 minutes away!

2 Use road map C on page 61 to find the distance from:
   a) Hope (on A488) to Beguildy (the distance across the catchment area of the college)
   b) Bishop's Castle to each of the other main shopping areas.

3 How many people, according to diagram D, shop in Newtown?

4 Why are people willing to travel so far to do their shopping? What problems does this create?

5 Use road map C on page 61 to sketch the route that an ambulance would take from Ludlow, to Bishop's Castle, to Shrewsbury.

6 *Describe in your own words the problems rural isolation can cause.*

▲ **C** *Farmers come from all over the area to the livestock market every Friday*

▼ **D** *Where people from Bishop's Castle do their shopping*

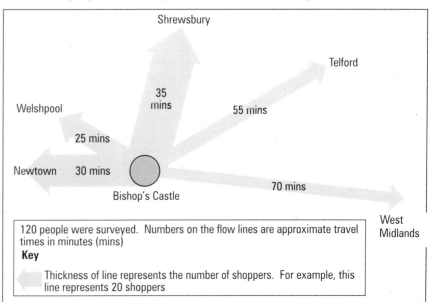

120 people were surveyed. Numbers on the flow lines are approximate travel times in minutes (mins)
Key

Thickness of line represents the number of shoppers. For example, this line represents 20 shoppers

Employment in the rural community

Changes in farming, as we have learned, have led to job losses on the farm. Finding a job in the countryside can be very difficult, particularly in isolated communities like Bishop's Castle.

A small business

Nick Downes is a self employed and highly skilled furniture maker. The small scale of his business means he can work from home in a workshop converted from a farm barn. He sells his handmade furniture all over the country, and some goes abroad. He employs Andrew, who is on a training scheme and who goes to college in Shrewsbury once a week.

A large business

Ransfords is a large and modern timber yard employing 56 people. The timber is dried and treated using a computerized process. It is the largest plant of its kind in the UK, and one of the largest in Europe. It processes 40 000 tonnes of timber a year.

The yard is in a good location because it can buy locally grown timber from the Forestry Commission. Most of it comes from Shropshire or Wales, within a 150km radius of Bishop's Castle. Ransfords supply timber products all over the UK. They are the largest producer in the UK of railway sleepers, and supply 90% of the UK's motorway fencing and 98% of the fencing used along main roads to screen traffic noise from nearby housing.

▲ **B** *Ransfords timber yard on the edge of Bishop's Castle*

1 How do these two work places compare with factories that you may have seen?

2 Use map C and an atlas.
  a) List the counties of Wales that have more than 15% forest.
  b) How many counties with more than 10% forest cover are within a 150km radius of Bishop's Castle?
  c) Why is Bishop's Castle an ideal location for a timber yard?
  d) Which other parts of the British Isles would be good locations for a timber yard?

3 What similarities and differences are there between Downes' furniture business and Ransfords? Consider size, why they are located there, mechanization, and where they sell their products.

▲ **A** *Nick Downes' workshop*

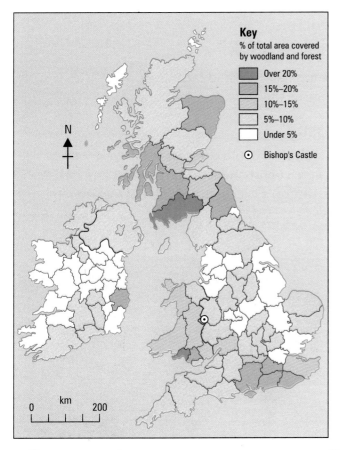

▲ **C** *Forestry in the British Isles*

The problem of attracting new jobs

The two largest employers in Bishop's Castle closed in 1993. About 150 people lost their jobs, which was 25% of all jobs in the town. Now, the two largest employers are the Community College and Ransfords Timber Yard. Bishop's Castle has difficulty in attracting new businesses to the area, as diagram D shows.

4 Why are Newtown and Telford more successful at attracting new firms than Bishop's Castle?

5 Imagine you work for South Shropshire District Council. Design an advertisement for a national newspaper which will attract firms to the area.

6 *Make a list of the kind of firms who might locate in a rural area. They might be firms who have a rural connection (like the timber yard), or firms that could locate anywhere (like the furniture business).*

▼ **D** *Why Bishop's Castle finds it difficult to attract new firms*

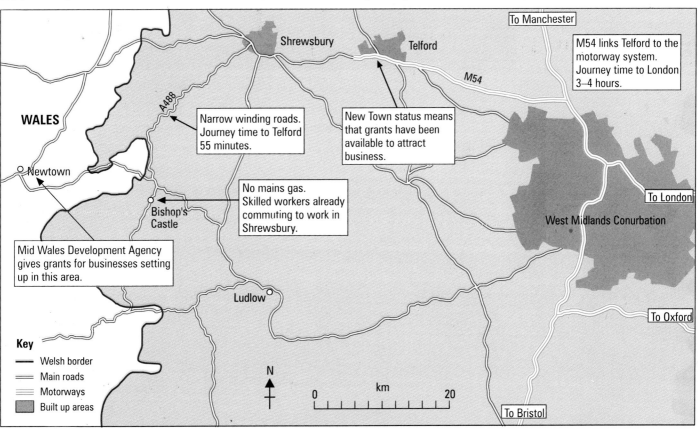

The rural community fights back!

- How can rural communities attract new jobs and facilities?
- How might the landscape change as the rural area continues to change?

Cashing in on the leisure industry

Many rural areas already attract visitors. People come to walk, cycle, or ride through the countryside. Others visit country houses, gardens, or farms that are open to the public. People in Bishop's Castle have different views on the effects of more visitors, as B shows.

▶ **A** *Footpath erosion on the Stiperstones*

1 Use photo A.

a) Discuss what people find attractive about this kind of countryside. Make a list.

b) If people are around 1.75 metres tall, estimate the width of the path.

c) Describe the path and suggest reasons why it is getting wider.

2 Read the opinions in B. Make a table of advantages and disadvantages of attracting more visitors to the countryside.

▼ **B** *Opinions on attracting more visitors*

We would love to have more visitors staying in the town. It would mean more money for the guest houses, the cafés, and gift shops.

I've converted my barn into holiday cottages. The money I make from renting them out will help make up for any loss of subsidies on the farm.

My furniture business might benefit. Local people would have more money to spend. People really only buy furniture if they have money to spare.

Having too many visitors can lead to traffic congestion in the narrow lanes, and parking problems. Some footpaths are already too heavily used. Plants are trampled and the paths become eroded.

New uses for old farm land

Farmers already try new crops, like the oilseed rape (see page 58), when the demand for traditional crops falls. Farmers in upland areas, such as the area around Bishop's Castle, might be tempted to plant trees if their subsidies were reduced. These trees could be coppiced (as diagram C shows) and the timber processed into fuel pellets. Such pellets can be burnt on home wood-burning stoves or used as fuel in rural power plants, generating electricity for the local community.

Telebureaux

Nowadays many jobs can be carried out almost anywhere, thanks to modern communications and technology. People can work from home, keeping in touch with an office using a fax machine or a computer connected with a telephone modem. Newspaper and magazine journalists, researchers, and editors can all work from home in this way.

A small office in a rural area, equipped with a computer, photocopier, and fax could be used as a central resource by a number of teleworkers. The equipment would also benefit other small businesses in the rural community, including local farmers.

3 Consider the impact of each of the three schemes outlined on:
a) local jobs
b) the countryside
c) traffic on local roads.

4 Write a report to South Shropshire District Council suggesting what you think should be done to boost jobs in the area. You could choose one or more of these schemes, or suggest an idea of your own.

Young trees are planted on poor grazing land.

The trees take five years to grow. They provide shelter for animals and birds.

The young trees are cut (coppiced). This encourages new growth from the stump.

Plants on the forest floor benefit from the extra light once the trees have been cut

Different areas of the woodland are cut in rotation to provide a steady supply of wood, and a wide variety of habitats.

▲ **C** *How a woodland is coppiced*

▲ **D** *The equipment needed in a telebureau*

Review

- Settlements of different sizes have different facilities.
- Each settlement serves a local catchment area.
- Rural areas are changing.
- Some traditional jobs have gone, but rural communities are adapting to the changes and offering new types of work.

7 Improving city life

2310 million people live in the world's cities. These cities are constantly growing and changing.
- **How different are cities around the world?**
- **How do different countries try to tackle their urban problems?**
- **Who benefits when cities change, and do they always change for the better?**

Through this unit we will be looking at cities in three different countries to see how they have coped with similar problems. Map A shows where these three cities are, and other major cities in the world.

▼ **A** *The world's wealth and major cities*

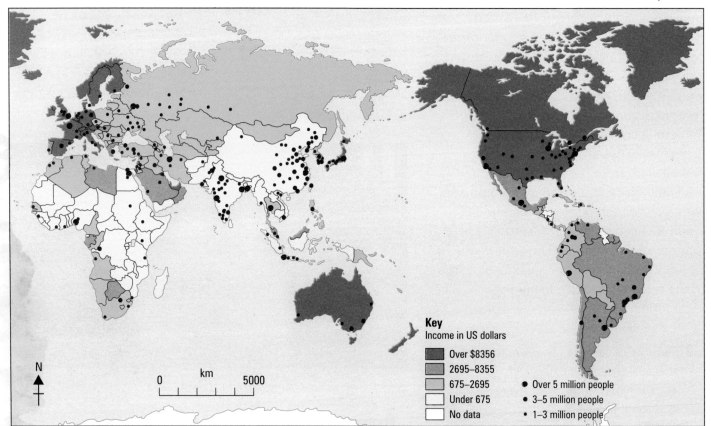

Key
Income in US dollars

- Over $8356
- 2695–8355
- 675–2695
- Under 675
- No data

- ● Over 5 million people
- ● 3–5 million people
- • 1–3 million people

N

0   km   5000

---

1 Copy out the statements that are true.
Correct the others as you rewrite them.
a) The UK is richer than Portugal.
b) Brazil has more cities with over a million people (millionaire cities) than India.

c) Most cities of over 5 million are in rich countries.
d) China has more millionaire cities, and is richer than the USA.

2 Use an atlas to find the names of all the cities shown in map A that have a population of over 5 million.

Hong Kong

Hong Kong is situated on the coast of southern China. It covers 1000km², but the city itself only covers about 50km². The rest is made up of a rural area (The New Territories) and numerous small islands.

Hong Kong is a modern, bustling city of 6 million people. It is a successful financial and manufacturing centre. Much of the city is built on a small island. Steep mountain sides have made it difficult for the city to expand.

▶ B *Hong Kong*

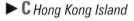

3 a) Describe how the land is being used in photos B and C. Use words such as:

housing   transport   leisure   business

b) In what other ways is land used in a big city? Try to give an example you have seen.

c) Is it a good idea to have all of these land uses mixed up in a small part of the city? Try to give one advantage and one disadvantage this might cause for local people.

4 Use photo C to describe how city planners have overcome the shortage of land.

▶ **C** *Hong Kong Island*

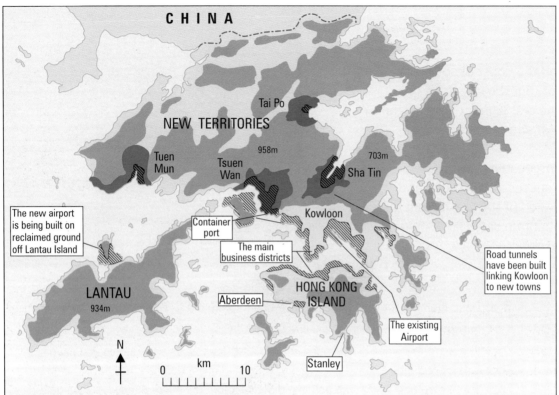

A *Hong Kong's main urban areas*

Key

Land over 250m

Urban areas

New towns
New towns have been built in the New Territories. These towns are full of government–owned tower blocks. The flats are cheap to rent.

Reclaimed land
Land has been reclaimed from the sea. Sand and rock is dumped in the harbour to create new flat land.

Improving Hong Kong

Like many other cities in the developing world, many people have moved to Hong Kong from the countryside to take advantage of the jobs and higher standard of living found in the city. The city planners have had three main tasks:

● to provide enough cheap housing
● to find space for building
● to keep the traffic flowing in this congested city.

How have the city planners tackled these problems?

Tower blocks have been built to save space. Hong Kong has the highest skyscrapers in south-east Asia. The average population density is 5559 people per km^2. Hong Kong is one of the most crowded places on the Earth. Some parts of the city have 105 000 people per km^2. Map A shows some of the other changes the planners have made.

◀ B *Central Plaza, the highest building in south-east Asia*

1 Using map A, answer these questions.
a) What is the length (east to west) and breadth (north to south) of the city on Hong Kong Island?
b) What shape is the city on Hong Kong island, and why?
c) What types of land use has the reclaimed ground been put to?

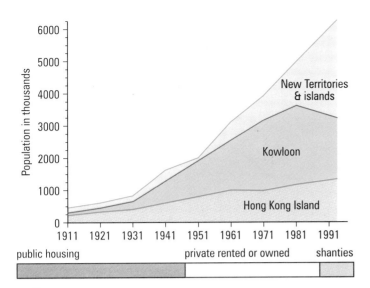

▲ C *Growth of population in Hong Kong and ownership of housing*

Public housing

The movement of people to Hong Kong led to the growth of **shanty towns**. These settlements have been built by ordinary people on land that does not belong to them. It is a common feature of developing cities.

In 1954 a fire swept through a shanty town in Kowloon, making more than 50 000 people homeless. After this, the government decided to knock down the shanty towns and provide proper housing. They have since built hundreds of high rise flats that people can rent cheaply.

The first blocks were badly designed and cheaply built. The flats were very small and people had to share the cooking and washing facilities. The flats in the recent tower blocks are larger and better designed.

▼ D *Opinions of shanty dwellers on the resettlement*

> The new flats look very nice, but I'm not sure I can afford the rent.

> I've always lived in Stanley. I've got a lovely house which I've built and improved over the years, and a small garden . I don't want to see it bulldozed.

> I work in the market in Stanley selling silk shirts to the tourists. It would be really inconvenient if I had to travel from Aberdeen every day.

▲ E *Modern high rise tower blocks in Sha Tin, in Hong Kong's New Territories*

▲ F *Stanley, one of the last remaining shanty towns on Hong Kong Island*

2 Describe the buildings in photo F. Where are they built, and what are they built from?

3 Compare the homes in F to the flats in E. What advantages and disadvantages does each type of home have?

4 Use graph C to find out what percentage of Hong Kong's population lives in:
a) public housing
b) shanty towns.

5 Do you think the Hong Kong government is right to force people out of the shanty towns? Imagine a discussion between someone who is against the resettlement and someone who is for it. What might they say to each other?

Changing Norwich city centre

Norwich is the main settlement in Norfolk and a regional centre for East Anglia. A hundred years ago the population of Norwich was 120000. Of these, 80000 lived inside the old city walls. Many factories and workshops were close to the river with housing that was often cramped and overcrowded.

Today 180000 people live in Norwich but the city covers a much larger area. Only 8000 people live inside the city walls. New housing estates and factories have moved to the outskirts. These changes can create problems in the city centre as buildings become empty and fall into disrepair.

1 **a)** In which county is Norwich?
   b) How far and in which direction is Norwich from:
   (i) Great Yarmouth
   (ii) Ipswich?

2 Summarize the main changes in Norwich city centre over the last 100 years.

3 Using map D, give directions for a car driver who is coming into Norwich on the A11, to park the car and shop in Gentleman' Walk.

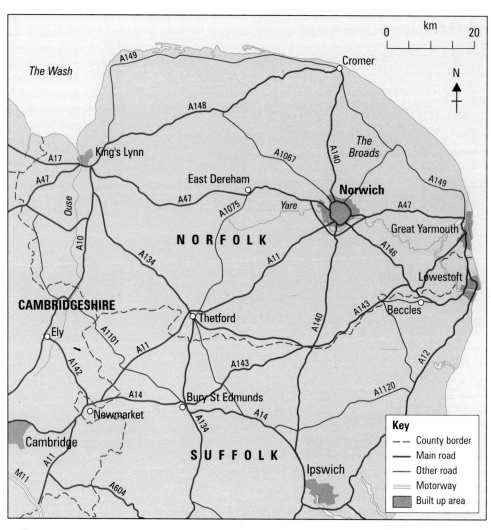

▲ **A** *Location of Norwich in East Anglia*

▲ **B** *Medieval street in Norwich*

Developing the city: pedestrianization

The streets in the centre of Norwich are very old and not designed for modern traffic. As more people use cars, the narrow streets become congested and dangerous. One solution is to ban cars from certain streets. This is known as pedestrianization. On the pedestrianized streets the council permits buskers and is encouraging street cafés. Pedestrianization has been opposed by traders in the past, especially street traders on market day, who were worried that their businesses would suffer if cars were banned from the streets.

▲ C *Pedestrianized city street in Norwich*

How successful was the scheme?

City planners carried out a survey to find out if the pedestrianization scheme had really been a success. They found:
- there were three times as many pedestrians
- 40% of pedestrians questioned said they came more frequently
- 25% of pedestrians stayed longer
- noise levels had been reduced
- levels of lead in the air had fallen by 66%
- fewer buildings were empty and many traders had refurbished their buildings.

Banning cars a success! claim city planners

Just a few years ago the Walk had 5500 vehicle movements a day. Today cars are banned and lorries are only allowed early in the morning or late in the evening. During the day the street is crowded with pedestrians and the roar of traffic has been replaced by the hum of conversation and the sounds of street musicians. Traders who campaigned against the change now admit they were wrong.

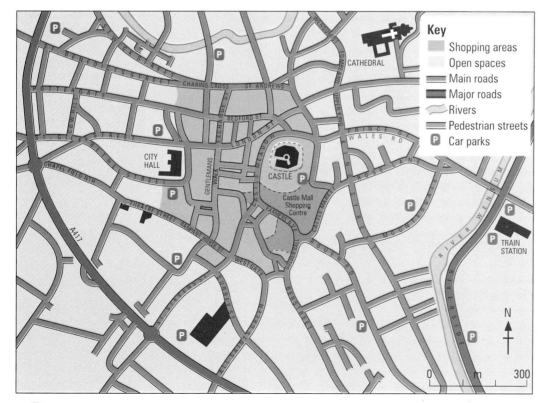

Key
- Shopping areas
- Open spaces
- Main roads
- Major roads
- Rivers
- Pedestrian streets
- P Car parks

▲ D *Norwich city centre*

4 a) Why were the traders worried about the pedestrianization scheme?

b) Why were buskers and street cafés encouraged?

5 Describe the effect that pedestrianization might have on:
a) disabled people
b) deliveries to the shops
c) emergency services.

6 What do you think was the biggest advantage of the scheme?

Developing a new shopping centre

In Norwich a large space by the castle was used as a car park after the cattle market moved to the outskirts. Some people wanted to see the car park turned into a green space but others felt that the city needed to develop a modern shopping centre there.

> I like the car park, it's very handy for the shops. We don't want any more change – it's spoiling the city. Norwich has lots of nice old buildings and a modern shopping centre wouldn't look right here.

> Norwich is far too congested, we need less cars in the centre so we should get rid of the car park. We should plant grass and trees so people can get away from the hustle and bustle. If we built a shopping centre it would attract even more cars. We should be making public transport better so people don't have to bring their cars into the centre.

> If people want a place to rest they can go to Cathedral Close or Chapelfield. The city needs a modern covered shopping centre where people can keep warm and dry. It's miserable walking round outside on a wet winter's day. They've built them in Ipswich and Peterborough. If we don't have one people will go there instead.

> We must preserve the old buildings and street patterns. Norwich is the largest medieval walled city in the UK. We have 4.5 million visitors to the city each year, bringing money and generating jobs.

> Norwich is used by 500 000 people from a large surrounding area. We need better facilities in the centre which people without cars can easily get to. There's a danger that we'll get a big shopping park on the edge of the city. If that happens the city centre will gradually die.

1 What are the advantages of:
  a) a covered shopping mall in the city centre
  b) a large out-of-town shopping centre on the edge of the city.

2 Imagine you are one of the following people. Write a letter to the Norwich council giving your opinion of the redevelopment scheme:
  a) a family who own a car
  b) the owner of a small shop in the city centre
  c) a pensioner who does not drive
  d) a teenager.

▲ **A** *Opinions on the proposed shopping centre*

Who won?

▼ **B** *The redevelopment site – can you tell what happened?*

Photo B shows what happened. The shopping centre was built under ground. It is known as Castle Mall. There are two shopping floors and a multi-storey car park. The large glass roof lets light into the shopping centre. The centre is used by 250 000 people every week. Owners of shops outside the mall say their sales have stayed the same or have gone up.

In 1995 the Castle Mall shopping centre won an award for good design. Ramps into the shopping centre make it easy and safe for the disabled and people with young children to use. The judges were impressed by the way Castle Mall fits into the historic town centre.

3 Look at the opinions in illustration A.
   a) Which of these people would be happy with the finished scheme?
   b) How did the scheme deal with the objections raised in A?
   c) Do you think that the development was a good idea? Explain your answer.

4 *Investigate the shopping facilities in your area. How might they be improved? Write a report which includes these headings:*

Location of the existing shops

A proposal for development/improvement

Possible impact of the development on:

* *the environment*
* *transport and traffic*
* *local people and traders*

Political changes and the city: Prague

In the 14th century, Prague was the second largest city in Europe. Because of its central position it was important for trade and culture. Between 1948 and 1989 Prague was the capital of communist Czechoslovakia, and the government owned nearly every building in Prague. In this case study we will answer important questions.

● What are the good and bad points of a city planned by the state?

● How has Prague changed since the communist government lost power in 1989?

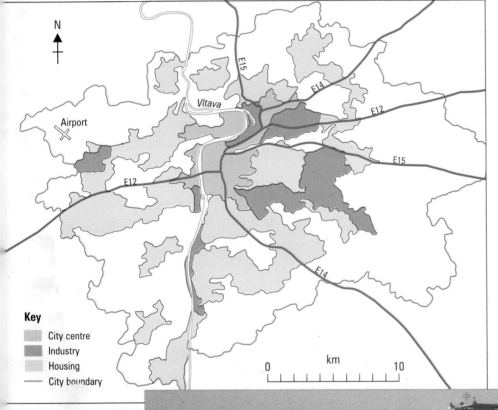

The communist city

The communist government of Czechoslovakia believed that everyone should have a fair deal in city life. During their years in control they changed Prague by building many blocks of flats. They were all built to the same design for speed and cheapness. Most blocks were built in three new towns on the outskirts of the city. The right to own property was taken away. Everyone had to rent their home from the government, at prices that were subsidized (kept low). An underground transport system was built connecting the new towns to the city centre. Fares were cheap. Also, part of the city centre was pedestrianized.

Key

▪ City centre
▪ Industry
▪ Housing
— City boundary

▲▲ **A**
The city of Prague today

▶ **B**
Blocks of flats built during the communist period

The Velvet Revolution

In 1989 the people of Czechoslovakia took power away from the communist government during a revolution so peaceful it was called the 'Velvet Revolution'.

The most important change since 1989 has been the return of the right to own property. In the old city centre 80% of houses have been given back to the previous owners, or their families.

However, 70% of people in Prague still live in flats, which remain government owned. Rents are no longer subsidized, and are now three times dearer than in communist days. The wages of most ordinary people have gone up only slightly.

Problems facing modern Prague

- Most flats built during communist control are heated by boilers that burn brown coal. The brown coal is rich in sulphur, and gives off sulphur dioxide, which causes acid rain.
- The excellent public transport system, and the high cost of petrol, have kept the number of cars in the city low. Only 20% of Czechs own a car. However, as car ownership rises, pollution and traffic congestion in the old city will become problems.
- Prague's water supply system is poor. About 30% of all water is lost from leaking pipes.
- The communist government did little to repair the city's many historic buildings and structures. Read the description of Charles Bridge in extract C, made by a visitor to Prague in 1979. After the 'Velvet Revolution', the planners had to decide whether or not to restore these historic buildings and structures.

The appearance of the Charles Bridge told us about Prague as it was then. A beautiful structure, famous for its life size statues that line the parapets on each side, the bridge was black with grime. It was just one of the sadder features of the city – crumbling buildings, peeling paint, air polluted by the stench of petrol and open drains. Prague was a neglected city with an air of hopelessness.

▲ **C** *Extract from* Nothing Ventured – A Rough Guide Special

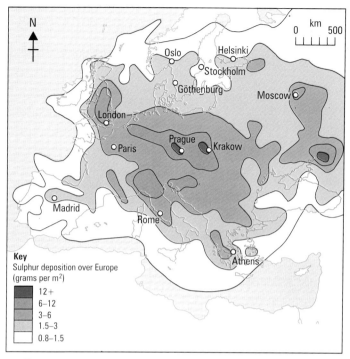

▲ **D** *Sulphur deposited in Europe*

Key
Sulphur deposition over Europe (grams per m^2)

- 12+
- 6–12
- 3–6
- 1.5–3
- 0.8–1.5

1 Use map A and the description of the communist city.
  a) In what parts of the city are the new housing estates?
  b) How far is it from the edge of the city to the city centre?

2 What did the communist government do to improve life for people in the city?

3 One problem facing many European countries is the pollution damage caused by sulphur deposition. How much sulphur is deposited in:
  a) Krakow and Prague   **b)** Paris   **c)** Madrid?
  d) Why is the problem particularly bad in Prague?

4 Look at the problems facing Prague. If you were a city planner, which would you make your priority? What would you do?

5 Both communist Prague and modern Hong Kong have tried to use similar planning solutions. Describe the similarities and differences you can see between the two cities.

Prague today

Czechoslovakia was split into two countries in 1993, and Prague is now the capital of the Czech Republic. Tourists, kept away by communism, are now flooding back to the city.

● What do the visitors find?

Prague was a cultural and commercial centre in medieval Europe. Beautiful public buildings, museums, art galleries, churches, and statues were built over the centuries. Many of these still stand in the old city centre and have been restored. The city attracts millions of visitors, as the factfile shows.

▼ **B** *The Charles Bridge in historic Prague*

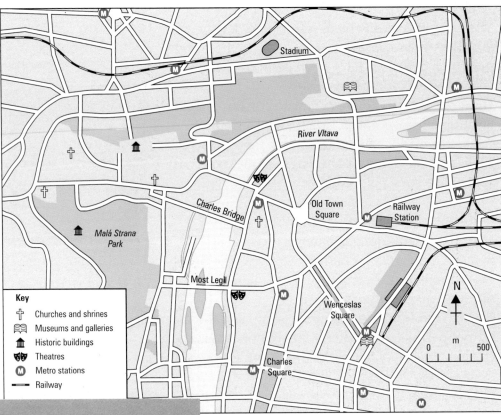

▼ **A** *Street map of Prague*

Key
- ✟ Churches and shrines
- 📖 Museums and galleries
- 🏛 Historic buildings
- 🎭 Theatres
- Ⓜ Metro stations
- ▬ Railway

Factfile: Prague

● Population: Czech Republic 10.42 million
Prague 1.26 million.

● GNP: US$2450 per person (about US $50 a week).

● In the Czech Republic as a whole, Prague has:

● 33% of all research and scientific activity

● 25% of services
(e.g. banks, education, office work)

● 14% of all Czech jobs

● 11% of population.

● 70 million tourists visited the Czech Republic in 1993 (more than went to France).

● Tourism earns the republic US $1000 million a year.

	Berlin	Brussels	London	Madrid	Paris	Prague	Rome	Warsaw
Berlin	—							
Brussels	780	—						
London	1170	390	—					
Madrid	2350	1550	1670	—				
Paris	1090	300	450	1250	—			
Prague	340	910	1310	2310	1000	—		
Rome	1490	1520	1810	2040	1400	1290	—	
Warsaw	560	1340	1730	2930	1620	620	1830	—

How is Prague changing?

Since 1989, all the communist-owned shops have been sold to private owners. In 1991, 1100 shops changed hands in six months. Many shops in the city centre have been bought by foreign firms. Some shops selling basic goods like food and clothes have closed down. Shops selling luxury goods have opened instead. New hotels and facilities for tourists, including banks, have opened.

◀ **C** *Road distances in kilometres between European cities*

I left Prague in 1968 and didn't return until early 1990 – shortly after the 'Velvet Revolution'. Since then I have returned twice, in 1990 and again in 1994.

In 1990 there were still food shortages. There was a craze then for bananas which were a novelty. People would happily queue for half an hour for a kilo of bananas. There were no adverts pasted up, and many things were the same as I remembered them in 1968.

In 1994 I saw many more changes. The run-down pubs I visited in 1990 have become smart wine bars. Locals can no longer afford to drink in them. The printers where I used to work has been replaced by a fast, efficient self-service supermarket. Food shortages are a thing of the past. There is now even a greengrocers called *Fruits de Paris* which imports fresh produce daily from France. Even the trams have changed. They still clatter through the cobbled streets, but instead of the distinctive red and cream colours, the trams are now covered in adverts.

▲ **D** *Roman, a Czech from Prague*

1 a) Discuss and list the reasons why so many visitors come to Prague. Map A and photo B will help.
b) Use table C to work out how far Prague is from:
 (i) Paris **(ii)** Berlin **(iii)** Warsaw.

2 Look at the factfile.
a) Draw divided bars to show Prague's share of research and service jobs.
b) Draw a divided bar to show Prague's share of the population.
c) Explain why Prague seems to have more than its fair share of research and service jobs.

3 a) List the changes in Prague since the 'Velvet Revolution', described by Roman.
b) Add to your list the changes described on page 77.
c) In what ways has life in Prague become better or worse since 1989?

4 *Use map A to plan an interesting route for visitors around Prague. Prepare a map and a short description of what the visitor will be able to see or do.*

Improving your own town or city

Hong Kong, Norwich, and Prague have all seen major changes in recent years. These changes have been made mainly by their councils or government. However, ordinary people can also bring about change in their neighbourhoods. The people of Gellatly Road, in south London, were so fed up about the amount of traffic using their road as a short cut, they decided to do something about it.

▼ **A** *Gellatly Road was used as a short cut*

> Cars were using our road as a 'rat-run', a short cut to avoid the traffic congestion on the A2. Residents' cars were always getting scratched and dented. Once a car went out of control and landed upside down in my front yard.

▼ **B** *Steve, one of the residents*

▼ **D** *Daily traffic flows in Gellatly Road*

1987

1993

= 2 000 cars

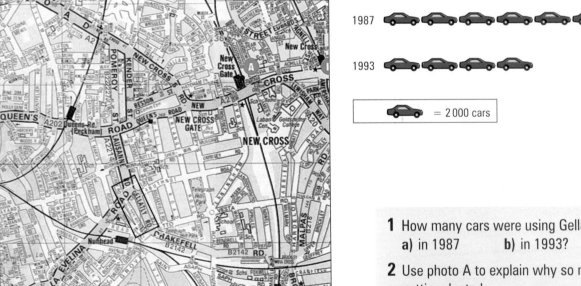

© Crown copyright

▲ **C** *Map showing Old Kent Road and Gellatly Road*

1 How many cars were using Gellatly Road:
a) in 1987   **b)** in 1993?

2 Use photo A to explain why so many cars were getting dented.

3 Why else would the local residents feel cross about the amount of traffic?

4 Draw a sketch map showing the route of the 'rat-run'. Label New Cross and Gellatly Road.

Changing the flow

A group of the residents formed a committee. They met regularly to discuss how the road could be improved. Cartoon E, below, shows what happened.

▼ E

1 A group of us crossed the road continuously during the rush hour one day.

2 Another day lots of us hired skips so that the cars would have to slow down to get down the road.

3 The man from the council met us. He said that if the road was closed, the cars would only cause a problem somewhere else.

4 Eventually speed bumps were installed. Higher up the road, pinch-points have been built. These have been very successful at slowing down the traffic and making our road a safer and quieter place to live.

5 Prepare a news report on the residents' action. Explain what they are doing and why.

6 Residents in other parts of New Cross are now complaining about increased traffic. Ambulance crews say they now take longer to travel through housing estates. Explain why each of these complaints may be linked to traffic calming schemes like the one in Gellatly Road.

7 *Investigate a local issue in your neighbourhood. You might survey the quality of the environment by:*
a) carrying out a traffic count
b) plotting the amount of green space and leisure facilities in the area.
You might use a questionnaire to find out what improvements local people would like to see.

Review

- Different cities suffer similar problems. These include: dealing with traffic congestion, and providing adequate housing for everyone.
- As cities change in response to these problems, some people benefit more than others.

8 The United States of America

The USA is a rich and powerful developed country.

- What gives the USA its distinctive character – its landscapes, people, and culture?
- How does the country vary from one region to another?
- How is the USA linked to the rest of the world?

▼ A   *Physical features of the USA*

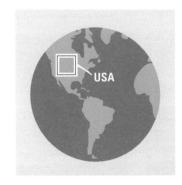

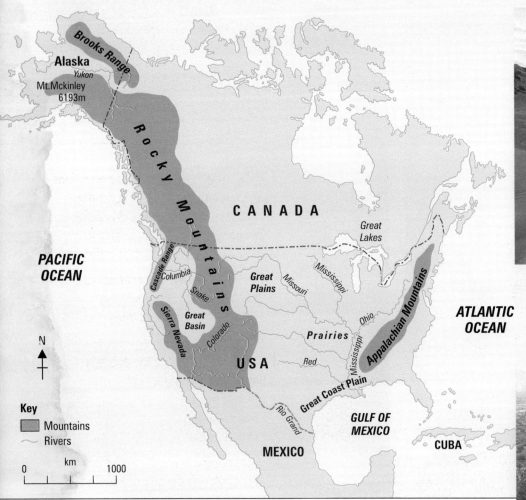

▲ B *The arctic climate of Alaska, USA*

▼ C *California has a hot desert climat[e]. Irrigated water has created this green landscape*

A big country

The USA covers 9.3 million km² and is divided into 50 states. You could fit the whole of the United Kingdom into it 38 times! It's so big it spreads across eight time zones – so when it is midnight in Hawaii it is 8 am on the east coast and 7 am in New York.

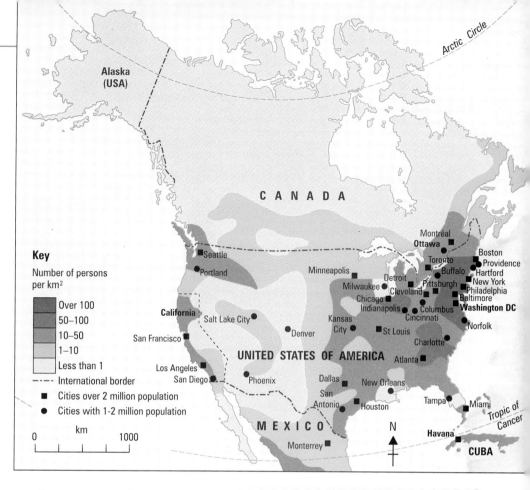

► D USA: population density and major cities

The American people

The USA is a relatively modern nation with a population of 257 million; only China and India have more people. Americans are amongst the richest people in the world, with an average income of US $22 560 (only the Japanese earn more, at US $26 920). Some parts of the USA have a much higher population density than others, and many Americans (75%) live in cities. New York (population 18.1 million) and Los Angeles (population 14.5 million) are two of the biggest cities in the world.

Key

Number of persons per km²

- Over 100
- 50–100
- 10–50
- 1–10
- Less than 1
- –·–·– International border
- ■ Cities over 2 million population
- ● Cities with 1-2 million population

km 0 — 1000

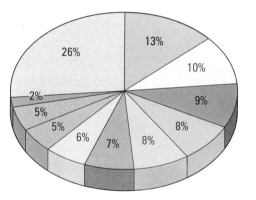

▲ E

The origin of migrants to the USA, 1820–1990

Key

- Germany 7 047 000
- Italy 5 333 000
- UK 5 064 000
- Austria/Hungary 4 322 000
- Canada 4 290 000
- Ireland 4 077 000
- Russia 3 433 000
- Mexico 2 802 000
- West Indies 2 520 000
- Sweden 1 281 000
- Others 14 259 000

(Pie chart values: 13%, 10%, 9%, 8%, 8%, 7%, 6%, 5%, 5%, 2%, 26%)

► F

Mike Peters USA

1 Using map A, answer these questions.
   a) Which river forms the boundary between Mexico and the USA?
   b) Name the mountain chains in the west and east of the USA.

2 Describe the housing in photo C. Consider house type, housing density, street pattern, and evidence of wealth.

3 Use map D. What is the average population density in
   a) Alaska
   b) New York
   c) Los Angeles?

4 Using photos B and C, explain why the population density of Alaska and Los Angeles, California are so different.

5 From which continent do most people in the USA originally come?

6 What is the message of cartoon F?

One country: many climates

The weather maps in A are from an American newspaper. They show how much cooler it is as one travels north across this huge country.

You would notice even bigger differences if you travelled across the USA during the winter. Compare the annual climate (chart B) for Chicago to that of Hawaii, the only American state in the middle of the Pacific Ocean.

▶ **A** *Weather for Alaska and the south-west USA taken from* USA Today *22 August 1994*

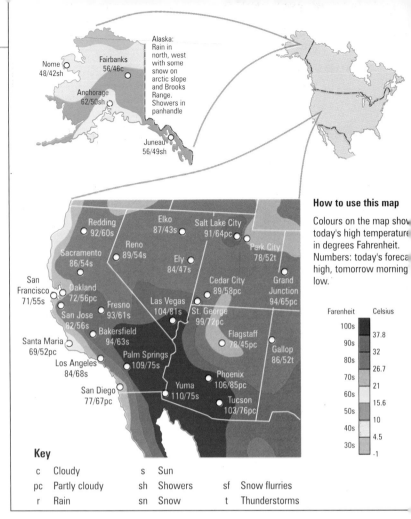

How to use this map

Colours on the map show today's high temperature in degrees Fahrenheit. Numbers: today's forecast high, tomorrow morning low.

Key

c	Cloudy	s	Sun		
pc	Partly cloudy	sh	Showers	sf	Snow flurries
r	Rain	sn	Snow	t	Thunderstorms

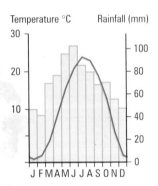
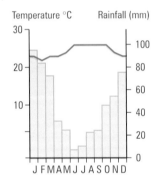

▲ **B** *Annual climate: Chicago, and Honolulu, Hawaii*

▼ **C** *Hawaii has a hot sunny climate*

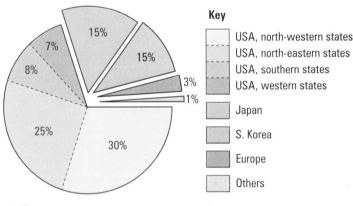

Key

- USA, north-western states
- USA, north-eastern states
- USA, southern states
- USA, western states
- Japan
- S. Korea
- Europe
- Others

▲ **D** *Where Hawaii's visitors come from*

1 Use the maps in A and the conversion scale to find the high temperature forecast (°C) in:
a) Nome   b) Anchorage
c) San Francisco   d) Palm Springs.

2 If you lived in Chicago, at what time of year would you like to visit Hawaii? Explain your answer.

3 Where do most visitors to Hawaii come from? Why do you think this is?

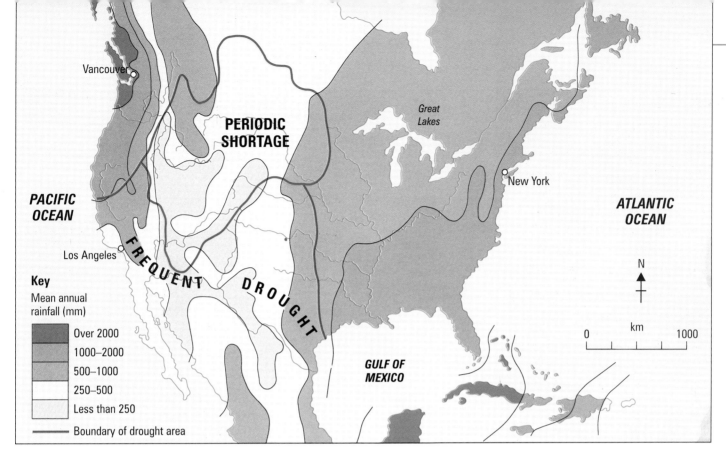

Key

Mean annual rainfall (mm)

	Over 2000
	1000–2000
	500–1000
	250–500
	Less than 250
——	Boundary of drought area

▲ **E** *Rainfall and regions of water shortage in the USA*

▼ **F** *The Glen Canyon Dam on the Colorado River*

Rainfall and water supply

Map E gives a further impression of the way in which climate varies from one region of the USA to another. Some regions are much wetter than others and, just as in the UK, this causes problems of water supply.

4 What is the total annual rainfall in areas of frequent drought?

5 Use an atlas to name two states which have:
   a) periodic water shortages   **b)** frequent droughts.

Colorado – the wild river

The River Colorado was once wild and powerful, carrying 80 million tons of sediment each year. The river carved out deep gorges and canyons, the largest of which is the Grand Canyon, 12 km wide, 1600m deep, and 349 km long. Melting snow from the Rocky Mountains swells the river each spring. Before dams like that in photo F were built, the swollen river would spill on to the flood plain, refilling ground water supplies, and spreading a layer of fertile silt on to the land.

6 Draw a sketch of photo F. Add the following labels:

Evidence of erosion   The dam
Power lines   Lake Powell

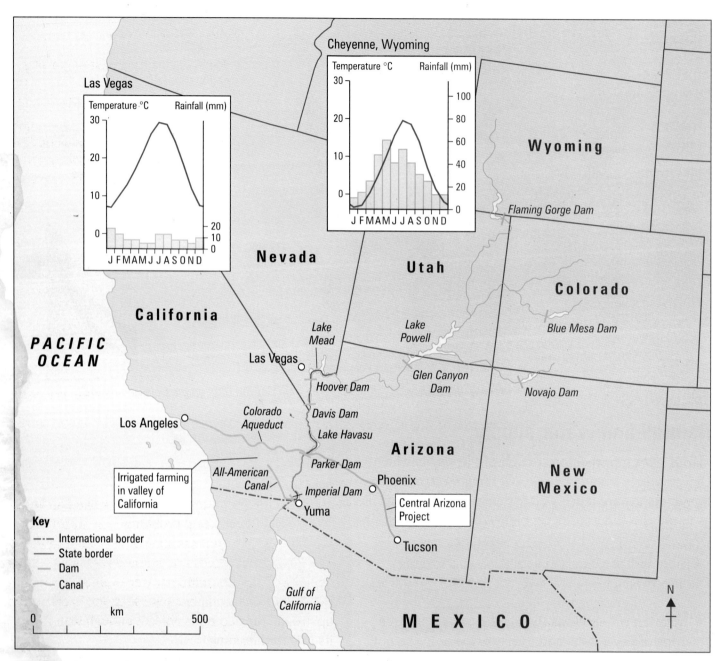

▲ **A** *The course of the River Colorado through south-west USA*

Harnessing the resources of the River Colorado

The US government began building dams on the River Colorado in the 1930s. The dams would generate cheap electrical power, and supply water to the rapidly growing cities of the desert states and the surrounding farm land. The dams would also control the flooding, and allow the river to be used for leisure and recreation. Twenty dams have now been built along the Colorado.

1 Study map A.
   a) List the states which the River Colorado flows through, starting at its source.
   b) Where does the Colorado reach the sea?
   c) Where do the following take the Colorado's water:
      (i) Colorado Aqueduct (ii) the All-American Canal
      (iii) the Central Arizona Project?
   d) How far is Tucson from the Parker Dam?

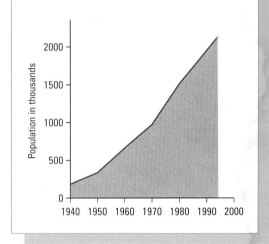

Factfile: Phoenix, Arizona

- Phoenix is the fourth fastest growing city in the USA.

- The city sprawls 80 km across the desert.

- Many factories have moved there, including high-tech firms making products such as computers.

▲ **B** *Las Vegas is the fastest growing city in the USA, partly because of the dams*

How successful have the dams been?

Advantages

- Water from the Colorado has allowed industries such as aerospace, computers, and engineering to move to the desert cities, bringing new jobs.
- The dams produce cheap hydro-electric power. HEP does not create pollution, and is a renewable source of energy.
- Irrigation water allows the growth of two or three crops of vegetables and fruit every year in the hot desert climate.
- Leisure facilities have been built along the river, creating thousands of jobs.

Disadvantages

- Increased demand for water in cities like Las Vegas and Phoenix is creating problems. The water table has already dropped because of over-abstraction. The River Colorado has no spare water left.
- Only 1% of the Colorado's water eventually reaches the Gulf of California because so much is extracted upstream. Mexico does not get enough water for its irrigated farming.
- Water is lost from the reservoirs and canals by evaporation. Some people believe that using water to irrigate golf courses and lawns is wasteful.

2 Look at the factfile.
   a) Describe the growth of Phoenix.
   b) Compare it to that of Hong Kong (graph C on page 71).

3 Why have cities like Phoenix and Las Vegas grown so fast? The information on this page, and page 19 will help. You should consider what makes these cities attractive to firms and to ordinary people.

4 a) Why has the water table dropped?
   b) How might the people of Las Vegas and Phoenix solve their water shortage problems?
   c) How might evaporation be prevented? (Look back to page 19.)

5 Has the development of the Colorado been a good or bad scheme? Explain your answer carefully.

Boom and bust, in the Great Lakes States

The Great Lakes area is a much older industrial region than the arid south-west. How has it changed over recent years?

▼ **A** *The Great Lakes states: position and resources.*

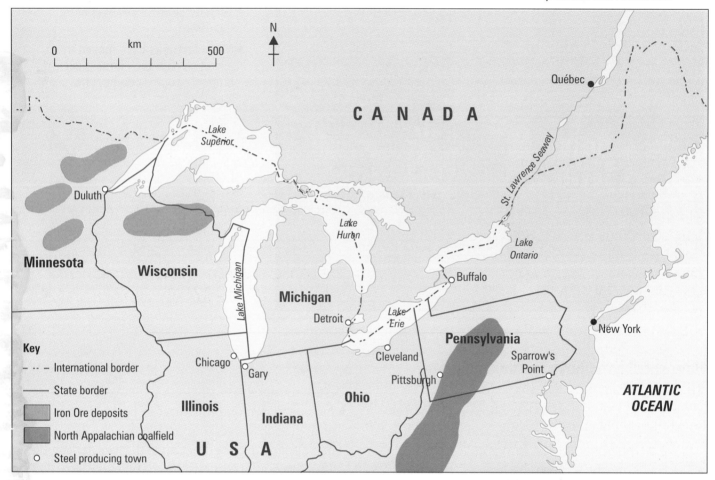

Key
- ‐ · ‐ International border
- —— State border
- ▨ Iron Ore deposits
- ▨ North Appalachian coalfield
- ○ Steel producing town

Early growth

In the 19th century the Great Lakes area became an important centre of steel making, coal mining, and engineering. In the 20th century, the car and steel industries brought jobs and prosperity to millions of people in towns such as Chicago, Cleveland, and Detroit.

▶ **B** *Ford car production line in the 1920s*

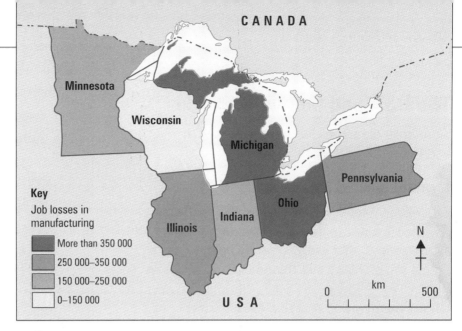

▲ C

Loss of jobs in manufacturing industry, 1977–92

The rust sets in

Factories closed during the 1970s and 1980s. Many people lost their jobs, and some moved away. The area became known as the Rust Belt because of the many derelict factories. There are several reasons for this decline in industry.

- Much of the equipment used in car plants and steel works became out of date.
- Higher wage rates and rising land costs made new firms look elsewhere.
- Cheap foreign cars imported from Japan competed with US cars.
- Countries such as South Korea, Japan, and Taiwan began to compete with the USA in overseas markets.

1 Using map A, answer these questions.
   a) How far is it from Chicago to Detroit?
   b) What natural advantages does this area have for steel making and the motor industry?

2 Study map C. Which two states lost most jobs between 1977 and 1992? What are their major cities?

Recovery in the Rust Belt in the 1990s

The region is now recovering. The US car industry has revived. Banking and insurance firms have been attracted to the area. Hi-tech firms have moved in with products such as medical instruments and computers. Foreign companies, like the Japanese car firm Honda, have built assembly plants in the region. Unemployment is falling. City centres are being redeveloped.

► D *Electric MFG plant, Chicago*

Factile: Peoria, Illinois

- Population grew by 7000 to 346 000 between 1987 and 1994.
- 2600 new jobs were created in 1993 alone.
- Local employers say it's easy to find skilled people who can repair machines and operate computers.
- An average house costs US $70 000, which makes it the eighth cheapest city in the USA.
- There are lots of new offices and factories with space to rent at low rates.
- A local office gives free advice about finding markets in Mexico and Canada.

3 What similarities and differences can you find between the two regions we have studied, the south-west and the Great Lakes? Concentrate on changes in jobs and in the cities.

4 Imagine that you have been given a 30-second slot on a US radio programme to tell firms why they should move to Peoria. Work in pairs to write a script which will highlight Peoria's advantages. Edit the script to cover all your points within 30 seconds, then record it.

The USA and the wider world

What links does the USA have with the UK and the rest of the world?

Tourism and leisure in Florida, USA

Every year, 8 million tourists from all over the world visit the USA. Many visit Florida, with its hot summers and mild winters, sandy beaches and theme parks. Many join the American visitors at Disney World, Orlando. Disney World is the world's largest theme park, covering 113 km² and receiving over 25 million visitors each year.

Spoiling the fun in Florida

The growth of tourism has created problems. Increased sewage is polluting the coast and threatening wildlife, especially the corals that grow in the only reef off the coast of the USA. Extract D shows how tourism has affected the fragile coral reef which runs for 220 km along the Florida coast.

►**C**

Visitors to Florida in 1993

▼**A** *The holiday resort of Miami, Florida*

▲ **B** *Route around Florida, from a travel brochure*

Country of origin	Number of visitors
USA	35 000 000
Canada	1 900 000
UK	1 137 000
Germany	454 000
Brazil	300 000
Venezuela	268 000
Mexico	230 000
Argentina	200 000
Columbia	127 000
Japan	112 000
France	110 000
Italy	85 000

The coral suffocates

At a depth of 10 m, where the coral suddenly rose in a ledge from the sandy ocean floor, it seemed that the entire reef had been wrapped in plastic string. This was fishing line, dozens of fishing lines, cast off by impatient anglers when their hooks caught in what they thought was the ocean floor. In fact, the hooks are locked into the soft coral. The results are devastating. Delicate sea fans tangled in line were pulled from the reef. Coral is wrenched off by the tugging from above. There were plastic bags looped over the brain coral, starving them of nutrients. Finally there were the great gouges in the reef where anchors had been dropped to moor the boats. It does not take an expert to see that a reef is dying.

▲ **D** *Extract from* The Guardian, *6 March 1990*

The export of American culture

You don't have to visit the USA to know about it. We all experience some part of American **culture**, almost every day.

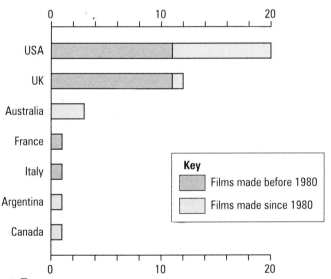

Key
Films made before 1980
Films made since 1980

▲ **F** *Origins of films shown on the four UK television channels in one week*

1 Look at map B. How far is Disney World (Orlando) from Miami airport?

2 Use the figures in Table C to draw a bar chart showing where tourists to Florida come from.

3 Write about Florida's attractions as though you were preparing a travel brochure.

4 Read extract D.
   a) What are the four main causes of damage to the coral?
   b) Why are tourists to blame?
   c) Design a poster for tourist fishing trips warning visitors of the damage they can do to coral.

▲ **E** *Familiar characters from Disney World, USA*

5 Using graph F, describe the position of the UK film industry (use figures from the graph to support your answer).

6 a) Make a list of all of the ways in which the USA influences our culture.
   b) Are all of these good influences? If not, what is bad?
   c) What aspects of our own culture should we try to preserve?

The USA and the Pacific Rim

From Europe's point of view, the USA is a close friend just over the Atlantic Ocean. However, the USA has links with other places, too. Much of the USA's trade is with the countries around the Pacific Ocean.

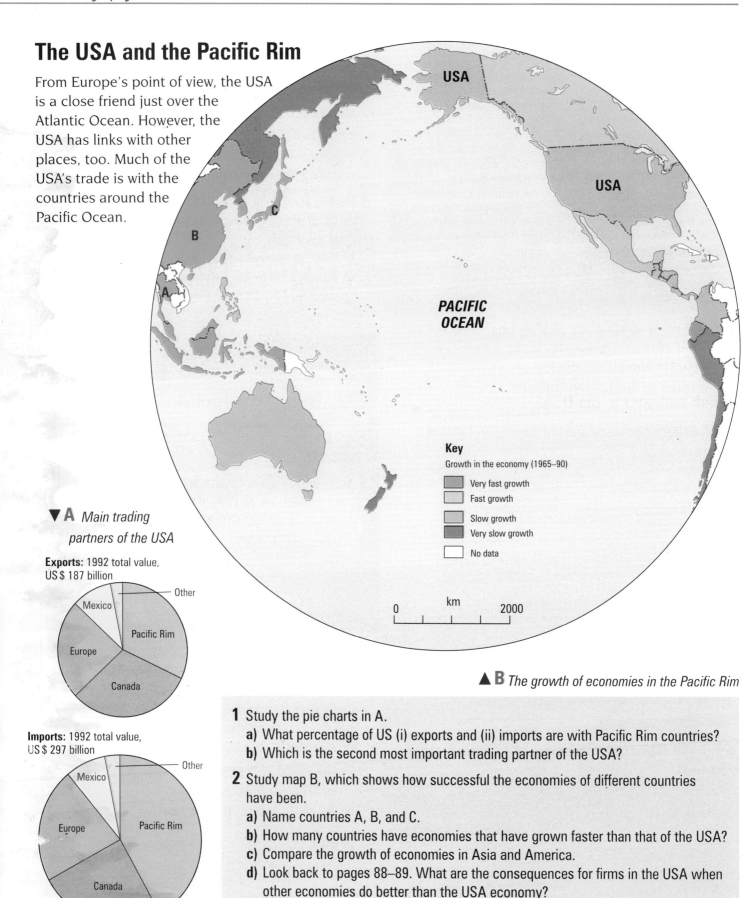

▼ **A** *Main trading partners of the USA*

Exports: 1992 total value, US $ 187 billion

Mexico — Other — Pacific Rim — Europe — Canada

Imports: 1992 total value, US $ 297 billion

Mexico — Other — Europe — Pacific Rim — Canada

Key
Growth in the economy (1965–90)

- Very fast growth
- Fast growth
- Slow growth
- Very slow growth
- No data

PACIFIC OCEAN

km
0 — 2000

▲ **B** *The growth of economies in the Pacific Rim*

1 Study the pie charts in A.
   a) What percentage of US (i) exports and (ii) imports are with Pacific Rim countries?
   b) Which is the second most important trading partner of the USA?

2 Study map B, which shows how successful the economies of different countries have been.
   a) Name countries A, B, and C.
   b) How many countries have economies that have grown faster than that of the USA?
   c) Compare the growth of economies in Asia and America.
   d) Look back to pages 88–89. What are the consequences for firms in the USA when other economies do better than the USA economy?

Review

The USA is made up of 50 states. Travelling across the states from coast to coast, or from Canada to Mexico, you see the changing character of the country. The landscape gradually changes, dividing the USA into a number of large regions, bigger than the states themselves. These regions are given their character by their climate and landscape, their people and their economies.

We have also seen that the USA is a powerful nation, rich in natural resources, skills, and technology. It is an important world power, some would say a super-power. However, its economy has not grown as fast as some other countries in the Pacific Rim during the last 25 years.

Rich and poor in the USA

Not everyone in the USA is rich. In 1991 there were 45 million people below the poverty line (US $15 000 for a family of four). Map C shows that some states have more poor people than others.

▲ D *Poor housing in Birmingham, USA*

3 Look at map C. Which region of the USA has most poor people?

4 From what you have learnt in this unit, compare and contrast two regions of the USA. Use the following headings: **Climate and environment People and economy**

▼ C *Percentage of families living below poverty level*

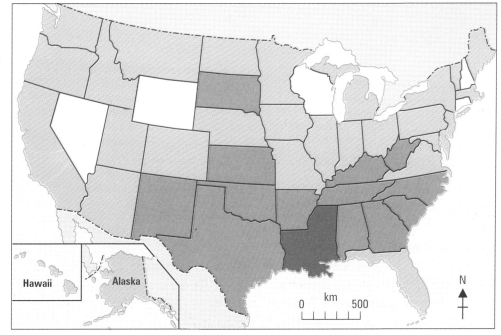

Key

% of population below poverty line by state

- 15.0–19.9
- 11.0–14.9
- 7.0–10.9
- Less than 7

Hawaii

Alaska

km
0   500

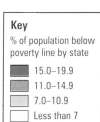
N

Glossary

Abstraction   The removal of water from a river or from the ground.

Aquifer   A layer of rock, such as chalk, which can hold large quantities of water.

Canyon   A deep, steep-sided river valley.

Catchment area   The area from which people travel to use a facility such as a school or shop.

Climate   The average weather conditions of a place or region. Daily weather records are added together and the average found to give a general pattern of climate over a year.

Community   A group of people who live close to one another and share the same local facilities. Plants and animals also form communities.

Condensation   Tiny water droplets formed as water vapour cools. Mist, fog, and cloud are formed by the condensation of water vapour in the air. Dew forms when water vapour condenses on the ground.

Confluence   The place where two or more streams or rivers join.

Culture   The customs, habits, arts, and religions of a community.

Dehydration   Loss of liquids from the body.

Delta   The area of low flat land at the mouth of some rivers where sediment is deposited. The river splits into smaller channels as it flows across the delta towards the sea.

Deposit   To drop sediment. Rivers deposit sediment on the inside bend of meanders, on their flood plains, and on the delta. The sea deposits sediment on the shore as a beach.

Desalinate   To remove salt from sea water for drinking and irrigation.

Desert   An area with less than 250mm of rain each year, and very little vegetation. Deserts can be hot or cold.

Developed countries   Countries with wealthy economies and a high percentage of people living in urban areas.

Developing countries   Countries with poorer economies and where many people live in rural areas.

Drainage basin   The area which is drained by a river and its tributaries. Also known as a catchment area.

Embankment   A river bank which is built up to prevent water from flooding on to the land next to it.

Environment   The surrounding in which people, animals, and plants live. It may be a natural environment such as rainforest, savanna, or an urban environment such as a city.

Equator   An imaginary line round the middle of the Earth which represents the 00° line of latitude. It is 40 076km long.

Erosion (Erode)   The wearing away of the Earth's surface by the action of rivers, ice, sea, or the wind.

Estuary   The mouth of a river where fresh water meets the salt water of the sea.

Evaporation   The changing of a liquid into vapour as it is heated. Water evaporates from the sea, lakes, and rivers to form water vapour in the air.

Flood plain   The flat land beside a river. Flood plains have sediment deposited on them during floods.

Glacier   A mass of ice. Most glaciers flow down valleys and erode the land as they go.

Gross National Product (GNP)   is a measure of the wealth of a country. It is usually divided by the population of the country, to give a rough idea of the average wage per person.

Hectare   An area of land equal to 100m × 100m.

Hydro-Electric Power (HEP)   Electricity produced by the force of fast-moving water. The power of the moving water is used to drive turbines which generate electricity.

Hydrological cycle   Another name for the water cycle.

Ice cap   Large area of snow and ice. Ice caps cover some mountain ranges and both poles.

Igneous rock   A crystalline rock that is resistant to erosion, such as granite.

Impermeable rock   A rock which does not allow water to pass through it, such as clay.

Irrigate   To transport water to an area where there is a shortage, usually for growing crops.

Latitude   Distance north or south of the Equator, as measured by imaginary lines around the Earth drawn parallel to the Equator.

Longitude   Distance east or west of the Greenwich Meridian (00 degree longitude) as measured by imaginary lines running around the Earth through both Poles.

Malnutrition   Inadequate nourishment as a result of poor diet, or lack of certain types of food. Malnutrition leads to illness and may lead to death or disability, especially in children.

Meander   A bend or curve in the course of a river.

Monsoon   A wet season of the year in southern Asia. Rainfall is highest during the summer months.

Mouth   The place where a river enters the sea, or a lake.

National Parks Areas of countryside that have been set aside for conservation and for leisure.

Nomads Nomadic people (nomads) who do not have a fixed home. They move from place to place in search of water and grazing land for their animals.

Permeable rock A rock which allows water to pass through it, such as limestone.

Pollution Contamination of water, land, or air by waste. Rubbish, sewage, industrial waste, exhaust fumes are all examples.

Population density The number of people per area of land.

Population distribution The pattern of where people live.

Precipitation Water, in any form that falls from the sky, including rain, snow, hail and sleet.

Renewable Renewable describes a resource that is not destroyed but can be used over and over again. Water is one example. Renewable energy is produced from sources that will always be available, such as wave power, wind power, and tidal power.

Reservoir A lake made for storing water.

Rural area Country area where most people live in villages and small towns.

Sanitation A sewage system and clean water supply.

Savanna A grassy plain with few or no trees found in tropical and subtropical regions.

Scale The size and detail in which something is seen. The more detail that can be seen, the larger the scale.

Sediment Pieces of rock which are carried and then dropped by water, wind, or ice.

Sedimentary rock Any rock formed by deposited sediment.

Settlement A group of houses and other buildings. It may be just a few homes or a large city.

Shanty town A squatter settlement, often on the outskirts of a city.

Source The starting point of a river or stream.

Squatter settlement A settlement which has been built by the people who live there on land that does not belong to them.

Tidal Affected by the high and low tides of the sea.

Transpiration The process by which plants give off water vapour into the air.

Tributary A small river or stream which flows into a larger river.

Tropical cyclones Violent storms which start over the sea in tropical regions. High winds, heavy rain, and large waves cause flooding and destruction in coastal areas.

Tropical rainforests Forests that grow near the Equator, where there is high rainfall and temperatures above 25°C. At least half the world's species of wildlife live in the rainforests. The largest rainforests are found in the Amazon Basin in South America and in Zaire, Africa.

Tundra Areas close to the Poles where little rain falls and where average temperatures are below zero for most of the year. Little grows there except for mosses and lichen. The ground is permanently frozen. Only the top few centimetres thaw in the summer.

Urban area A built-up area, town or city.

V-shaped valley A valley with steep sides in the shape of a V, usually formed by river erosion.

Water cycle The process by which water falls on the Earth, and eventually forms rain again.

Weather The conditions of the atmosphere, such as the temperature, amount of rain, or sunshine.

Weathering The breaking down of rocks caused by the effects of the weather and atmosphere.

Index